Succeeding with OKRs in Agile (2nd edition)

How to create & deliver Objectives Key Results for teams

Allan Kelly

Succeeding with OKRs in Agile (2nd edition)

How to create & deliver Objectives Key Results for teams

Allan Kelly

ISBN 978-1-912832-30-9

Leanpub

Contents

Praise for the first edition

"Allan's writing is perfect for busy managers who need to set objectives and form initiatives that satisfy diverse stakeholders. Plus, it doesn't sugar-coat OKRs – they are part of a management system – not a medicine. Overall, a wonderfully concise and easy to read guide to using OKRs. Highly recommended." Russ Lewis, CxO coach

"Having read other books that argue strongly for OKRs as a panacea to achieve a high-performing organization, the perspectives here from Allan are balanced, informed by lived experience and provide patterns and anti-patterns to watch for. Insightful and powerful – thank you Allan for sharing such well-considered feedback." Richard James, Accenture

"This book is full of great insights and guidance around OKRs backed by multiple real examples that will be helpful in a number of domains... With OKRs increasing in popularity and numerous 'experts' emerging, save yourself the time and effort reading the wrong material and grab a copy of this book to learn more about the right ways to approach OKRs." Nicolas Brown

"This is absolutely brilliant book. If you really want to learn more regarding OKR in Agile and other important stuff related to it you must read this book. It's truly a master piece." N Mehta

"Super easy to read, with clear chapter summaries. Lots of solid content that is not hidden amongst fluff. Straight to the point and a must have for any agile practitioner curious about OKRs." Amazon buyer

"Allan has written plenty of good books, but this might be the best. It's certainly immediately useful to any team adopting OKRs. Whether you're just starting out or have been using OKRs for months, there's a wealth of hints, tips, heuristics and advice in this book." Seb Rose, Agile Coach

"This book, having established in its opening section the value of an OKR-driven approach, devotes the bulk of its focus to practical guidance which cuts through the all too common confusion most of us encounter when actually writing and working with OKRs. The forewarnings section in particular provides refreshing advice for making OKRs work for you." Ewan Milne, Agile Coach

Free book when you subscribe

Be the first to hear of Allan Kelly's latest articles, books, events and insights, and receive discounts on workshops – subscribe now[1].

Plus receive a free e-book – currently *Continuous Digital*[2] – when subscribing[3].

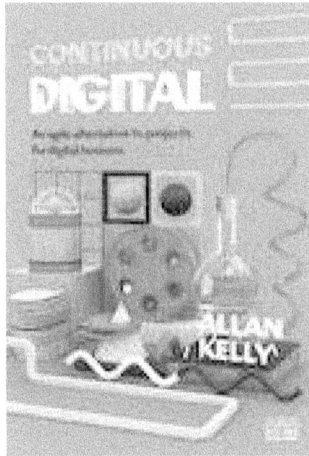

Continuous Digital

[1]http://allankelly.net/newsletter
[2]https://amzn.to/47HExTu
[3]http://allankelly.net/newsletter

Foreword

What a timely book! It comes at a time of global pandemic, with severe consequences not only for health and prosperity, but also for how we relate to each other and how we work. To the agile context of this book, a truly celebration-worthy 20th anniversary comes amid some serious self-scrutiny.

Agile's issues aren't so deep-rooted that they aren't fixable, but they are serious enough to need to be confronted before the disillusionment turns into crisis. Summarizing, I identify three key problems.

Problem one: orientation. We're seeing a divergence in the agile community represented, not so much by framework choices, but by what might be called 'drive' or 'orientation'. It's between heavily backlog-driven styles on one hand and deliberately outcome-oriented approaches on the other. In the worst examples of the former, teams are ploughing through backlogs of requirements with minimal opportunity for feedback, the team's experience and the customer's eventual results being no better than mediocre. Hardly agile at all by any useful definition, but with enough of its trappings to cause lasting damage to agile's reputation.

Problem two: autonomy. This problem is partly a consequence of the first, and it's a growing tension between team autonomy – something fundamental to agile – and strategy. As I have written elsewhere, it's a funny kind of autonomy when strategy is something that happens to you, but when all of your work is represented by a backlog over which you have little control this is very much what it feels like. Similar feelings of disempowerment and disengagement are triggered when ways of working move out of the team's control, the oh-so-ironic result of agile being implemented through the traditional rollout project.

Problem three: organization. The temptation to scale up agile processes is ever-present, but to do so without paying careful attention to other crucial aspects of organization design is fraught with difficulty. One specific manifestation of this problem is strategy dressed up in agile terms but still formalized hierarchically as work breakdown structures. This practice not only amplifies problems one and two, it adds a third: the inability of teams, departments, business units and management each to express themselves in terms appropriate to their respective domains. However elegant and convenient these structures might appear on paper, in practice they turn out to be unwieldy and oppressive, massive impediments to the kind of rapid feedback, learning and adaptation that businesses seek when they are encouraged down this path in the first place.

This book is unique in how directly it demonstrates how Objectives and Key Results (OKR) address these very real problems. Instead of teams ploughing through backlogs of requirements, they pursue meaningful objectives one key result at a time, an approach that is naturally outcome-oriented, iterative and adaptive. Instead of strategy being imposed on them from the outside, teams maintain in the form of OKRs their best understanding of how to meet the needs of their customers and other stakeholders. Instead of cascading hierarchies of objectives, mutual accountability and transparency act as enablers of self-organization and learning at every scale.

So it's all rosy then? Well, not so fast. OKR is not a million miles away from top-down Management by Objectives (MBO), a framework so plausible and yet so prone to devastating dysfunction that Peter Drucker, its highly respected creator, disowned it. It turns out that OKR is very much like agile; approach it from the wrong direction and some seriously bad things can happen.

Allan's treatment of OKR in this book isn't just enjoyable and practical (and I assure you that it is both), it stands for MBO's polar opposite. OKRs here aren't top-down, they are bottom-up, starting at team level and managed within an alignment process. They're expressed in each team's own words, the needs of others taken respectfully into account. Most dramatically, they change fundamentally how teams regard their backlogs. I shall leave it to Allan to explain that last one, but let me say now that as a long-time and vocal champion myself of outcome-orientation, I applaud his boldness.

There is more than one way to do agile, more than one way to do OKR, and multiple ways to combine them. Some of those combinations have enormous potential, and to anyone interested in exploring this exciting space I wholeheartedly recommend Allan's book. Well done my friend!

Mike Burrows January 2021, Chesterfield, Derbyshire UK

Founder, Agendashift agendashift.com[4]

Author, Agendashift: Outcome-oriented change and continuous transformation[5] (2nd edition March 2021)

Author, Right to Left: The digital leader's guide to Lean and Agile[6] (2019, audiobook 2020)

Author, Kanban from the Inside[7] (2014)

---

[4]https://www.agendashift.com/
[5]https://www.agendashift.com/books/agendashift-2nd-edition
[6]https://amzn.to/2NRZSoP
[7]https://amzn.to/3tqzsuy

Preface

This book is the product of Covid-19. What started life as some notes to myself on experiences using OKRs blossomed into a book during the first few weeks of England's first lockdown. Therefore, while one does not wish to dwell on Covid, it seems justifiable to write a few words about the lessons of Covid as they pertain to OKRs, and consider how OKRs can assist in this new world.

I am sure there were no risk logs in January 2020 that read 'World pandemic: international travel suspended; workers confined to home'. Few organizations were prepared for what happened in March, but few disruptions demonstrate the value of agility so clearly. Indeed, even those that would not consider themselves agile had to reshape their working environment literally overnight.

Urgency begat purpose: 'stay alive, stay productive'. Purpose begat focus: everything nonessential was pushed to one side, while entire companies pivoted to home working. Success was measured not in money spent, not in the time it took, but one single outcome: survival – the ability to continue operations.

Purpose, focus, outcomes: those three nouns could themselves summarize OKRs. When setting OKRs teams need to draw on their purpose, their raison d'être – their reason for being.

Once set, OKRs should be the focus of all work: *don't get out of bed in the morning if it doesn't contribute towards the OKRs*. OK, that's a slight exaggeration.

Focus, however, is only a means to an end, an outcome. More specifically, an outcome that moves the whole team – indeed the whole organization – along the path to fulfilling its purpose. Thus, while that purpose is front of mind when setting OKRs, outcome is central when judging success or failure.

> *Did the outcomes advance our purpose during the period of the OKRs?*

Whether OKRs are met or not is almost secondary. OKRs are a hypothesis for the coming quarter, a best effort guess at what will advance purpose. At the end of the quarter, review and adapt – what could be more agile?

While the response to Covid-19 has demonstrated the key qualities OKRs espouse, that response itself is the result of the digitization of human life and world commerce. What if Covid-19 had struck 20 years ago? Back in 2000 the world could not have locked down and shifted to home working the way it did.

Cell phones, the internet, Amazon and UPS all existed then, but not at the same scale, omnipresence or power. Back in 2000 few people had broadband internet, and online shopping – from home at least – was slow. Except for a lucky few, fast internet and video conferencing still only existed in the office. Had Covid struck in 2000 the economic damage and death toll would have been far higher.

And 20 years earlier still, 1980? Locking down for three months would have killed the economy. NTT launched the first cell phone in 1979, ARPANET became the internet in 1981, the same year IBM launched the PC, and TCP/IP was standardized the following year. A response to Covid-1980 would have looked a lot more like Spanish Flu 1918.

Digital made Covid-19 possible. Or rather, digital technology allowed the response that followed: the economy continued from home. The question nobody yet knows the answer to is: *to what degree will life return to pre-Covid ways?*

While each of us wants this awful illness gone and our old lives back, positive things have arisen from the crisis – this book for one. It is hard to see employers and employees reverting to office working without also supporting home working; some aspects of telemedicine will stay; Amazon and Netflix will retain new customers.

Depending on which commentators you listen to, Covid has accelerated the digital revolution by between five and ten years. It is clearer than ever that digital is here to stay. Both OKRs and agile have a role to play in this new world.

To start with, agile is the process change that accompanies digital. Agile is both the result of early digitalization – programmers received digital tools first and then invented agile – and agile is the way of working that accompanies digital tools. Nobody in their right mind tries to become a digital enterprise by writing a requirements document and building a Gantt chart. Digital demands agile.

Purpose, focus and outcomes become even more important when teams are distributed. Managers can no longer practice *management by walking around*, or even by watching staff. Managers must look at outcomes. Meanwhile, employees must redouble efforts to focus if working from a bedroom, especially with home-schooled children running wild! And everyone must share a purpose.

Digitalization means businesses are digital – or at least growth businesses are digitally driven – which means 'the business' is intimately coupled to the software. *The business is technology, and the technology is the business.*

For a digital business to change and grow, so too must its software. The idea that a software project can ever be 'finished' is a fantasy. When the software stops changing, so too does the business.

Businesses run on software products, not projects. This means the management model must change. IT is no longer a cost centre *over there* that 'does projects' that are always delivered late. Digital is as fundamental as accounting or marketing, and digital work is continuous.

There are those who see OKRs as a reinvention of projects. They see them as a command-and-control tool used by managers, they see them as a form of requirements document and they see the same goal-displacement failures.

I don't see them this way. OKRs fit well with the continuous agenda[8]. That book sets out an alternative vision.

OKRs provide a link to the 'bigger picture' – the purpose, the mission: they step up from sprint-sprint-sprint. Managers have influence in deciding what will be worked on, as they are entitled too: they are also stakeholders. Managers play a role in delivering OKRs, but managers are skilled in managing. None of that means managers can or should be using OKRs to boss a team about. Rather, OKRs are a mechanism for teams and managers to co-create shared goals that deliver beneficial outcomes.

During the 20 years since the agile manifesto many agile advocates, myself included, have at times felt as if agile has lost its way. There are places today that claim to work 'agile', but when old hands like me look at them they seem to be doing some watered-down version of agile that lacks any ambition to be better.

OKRs have the potential to reawaken the early ambition and drive inherent in agile. This time managers can join in too, not as obstacles to change, or change drivers, but as partners focused on the same outcomes for a greater purpose.

Allan Kelly, London, December 2020.

---

[8] Allan Kelly, *Continuous Digital*, 2018

Preface to the second edition

Rereading the first edition I surprise myself. I realise many ideas I had for changes were there already, albeit sometimes in prototype. So, *why a second edition?*

Well, books can always be better, the writing clearer, the ideas crisper. But one has to draw the line somewhere and *ship it.*

Books can always be longer and cover more material. I originally wrote several more chapters for *Succeeding with OKRs in Agile* that never made it into the final version. Adding chapters does not necessarily make a book better. As I often say, "The longer a document is, the less likely it is to be read", and "The longer a document is, then – if it is read – the less it is remembered." *Less is more.*

So additions are deliberately limited. The curious may like Succeeding with OKRs in Agile Extra[9], which contains these chapters, additional essays and posts. One day *Extra* might be finished in its own right; until then the draft is available on LeanPub and in a state of flux.

So why a second edition – what is different?

After I finished the first edition I continued learning, talking about the book, talking to teams, observing and listening to others. Now I want to share that learning and understanding.

The majority of changes concern planning and key results. The discussion of both has lead to new chapters and some refactoring.

The key driver for changing both was seeing *key results* more clearly as *acceptance criteria.* Key results are – well – *key*: important, crucial, fundamental, and *results* – outcomes, consequences, a description of the world. While the first edition advocated this view with experience I wanted it to be clearer.

The more I worked with OKRs, the more I have heard from others about OKRs, the clearer it has been to me that *key results are the difficult bit.* People struggle with key results more than anything else.

To be fair, one might say that opinion is divided. Authors differ in their advice on OKRs. Even some of the most authoritative texts on OKRs give examples I would not recommend now. I am also sure that in the past I have written OKRs with key results that I would disapprove of today.

---

[9]https://leanpub.com/agileokrsextra/

To square this circle I've outlined four different approaches to key results. I recommend that you avoid seeing key results as small pieces of the objective that are joined to make the complete thing. Rather key results are attributes of the target outcome that describe it – they describe the parameters the completed objective will meet. They might be constraints on the outcome ('Weighs less than 10kg'), sometimes they describe constraints on the input ('Costs less than $100 to manufacture'). Key results are, in agile terms, *acceptance criteria*. Which nicely furthers the idea that OKRs are *test-first management*.

Put it another way: objectives are not epics that are broken down into small pieces called 'key results'. Rather, objectives are akin to big stories – *business beneficial outcomes* – and key results are the acceptance criteria those stories should meet.

Reducing objectives and key results to an exercise in mereology means that key result writing becomes an exercise in work breakdown. That in turn means the OKR-setting becomes work planning. Consequently discussion of the production process displaces a focus on outcomes and customers.

Much else becomes easier when key results are interpreted as outcomes and acceptance criteria. OKRs cease to be glorified to-do lists and cascading OKRs become nonsensical. Key results as acceptance criteria might be harder to write, but doing so increases team freedom and options.

One example is in this book itself. Having a clearer perspective of key results allowed me to revisit the discussion of OKR-setting and planning. Under this view it becomes clear that OKR-setting is not work planning. Rather there is a two-step process: set OKRs, then plan delivery. Calling this out makes the whole setting/planning discussion clearer.

Revisiting these chapters also allows me to revisit the question of OKR cycle length. Notice I say 'OKR cycle', not 'quarter'. While there is the convention that OKRs operate on a quarterly cycle – three months, 13 weeks – this is not set in stone. I have come to see merit in both longer cycles, 16 weeks say, and shorter cycles, say ten weeks.

Today I see OKRs creating the opportunity for a new style of agile: *Objective Driven Agile*. Teams coordinate through interfaces called OKRs, backlogs only exist to meet an objective and are then discarded, planning is driven by those objectives and "How long will it take?" gives way to "How close can we get?".

But rather than lengthen this book further, *Objective Driven Agile* must wait for another day.

Allan Kelly, London, August 2023.

Short quick lessons

Bottom up

Don't impose OKRs from above. Don't set OKRs top-down.

Do set OKRs bottom-up. Allow each team to set their own OKRs to meet bigger goals.

Do let OKRs trickle up from the bottom.

Leaders should describe the ultimate goal, paint a picture and sketch out the future they want to make happen. Then let teams decide how they can make that future happen.

Every senior leader and layer of the organization has a duty to make those dependent on them successful.

Organization

Do make everything subservient to OKRs. Throw away the backlog.

Don't attach names to specific objectives or key results: OKRs are a team sport, not a list of an individual's tasks.

Don't manage dependencies. Do eliminate dependencies.

Rather than create a complex OKR-setting process to manage interdependencies, seek to remove dependencies. Enhance independence even at the cost of redundancy and duplication, strip away insulation layers and help connect teams with customers. In other words, increase cohesion and reduce coupling.

True north

Objectives are outcomes you wish to bring about.

Do use OKRs to guide you and fight to stay on course.

Don't change or abandon OKRs during a cycle without a fight.

But...

Don't stick blindly to OKRs as the world around changes.

Do talk to the whole team and get agreement before going *off-piste*.

If you find that your goals regularly change over a quarter, try working in short cycles. If the rate of change is too much, and is valuable, then write OKRs that demonstrate the value of continually changing goals.

Remember that if you always prioritize firefighting over pursuing goals, you will only ever be a firefighter. Firefighting is a very respectable profession but not everyone is, or should be, a firefighter.

Leaders

Do build *psychological safety* and *make failure an option*: only when it is safe to try, fail and try again will people be ambitious.

Do make it completely clear what the organization's priorities are.

Do make yourself available to teams, to answer their questions and answer them quickly.

Remember: teams only have a few weeks to deliver OKRs, so don't dally.

Do make resources available to the team or explain the constraints they must work within.

Do make clear the level of OKR achievement teams should be aiming for. If it is 70%, make that clear. If it is 80% or 60%, then make it even clearer.

Remember: OKRs belong to the team; you cannot tell them what to put in their OKRs.

Reviewing

Do practice *tough love* when reviewing OKRs.

Openly acknowledge you are doing so and recognize the need for psychological safety in the review process.

Ask questions such as:

- How does this create value?
- How will this be measured?
- Are these goals ambitious enough?
- Are the goals too ambitious?
- Are OKRs proving useful? Or are they getting in the way of real work?

Watch for signs that the team fear failure and lack psychological safety.

Team

Do make the team responsible for setting their own OKRs and delivering them.

Within the team Product Owners are first among equals when setting priorities: their work, skills and experience gives them insights into what customers want and value.

Teams that consistently achieve very high levels of OKR completion, or very low levels (say above 90% and below 50% respectively), deserve attention.

- Regularly hitting 90%+ of OKRs might lack ambition or, more likely, fear failure.
- Regularly missing OKRs by a wide margin might be a sign of over-ambition or failure to focus. More likely it is a sign of leadership failure or an organizational structure that does not adequately support the team.

Money

Do not link OKRs to bonuses and renumeration.

Just don't.

3 Questions

Whether you are about to begin your OKR journey or already in flight there are three questions, and answers, you should agree with you team and stakeholders. If you are working agile these questions are:

- **Which comes first: Backlog or OKRs?**

  Does the backlog drive the OKRs, or the OKRs drive the backlog?

- **Where does *business as usual* fit in?**

  When asked to do something important that does not directly relate to an OKR do you reply: "I'm sorry, OKRs take priority", or "OK, I'll do the OKR later" ? This is particularly important for teams covering *DevOps*.

- **Which is more important: predictability or ambition?**

  Do your stakeholders place higher value on predictability or on ambition, even if the team falls short?

Even if you are working in a less agile, more traditional style these questions are still relevant. The first question generalizes to "Which comes first: the work manifest/requirements or OKRs?"

Ultimately all three questions pertain to the priorities applied to your workflow. This book aims to help you answer these questions, and suggests my own answers.

I Why OKRs

One's philosophy is not best expressed in words; it is expressed in the choices one makes.

Eleanor Roosevelt, political figure, diplomat and activist, 1884–1962

1. Introducing OKR

Simple can be harder than complex: you have to work hard to get your thinking clean to make it simple. But it's worth it in the end because once you get there, you can move mountains.

Steve Jobs, 1955–2011, cofounder and CEO Apple Computer

OKRs = *Objectives* and *key results*: obvious, perhaps.

OKRs are about goals. Objectives are big goals, while key results are attributes of that goal. Sometimes they might be interim goals on the path to big goals, but more often they are descriptive of the objective. The question is, *how ambitious do you want to be?*

Make your objectives too big and ambitious and you might miss. Make your objectives small and easily achievable and you will hit them, but will they be as satisfying? Satisfying to you? Satisfying to your organization? Its a risk–reward calculation: you decide.

Goals bring focus, and focus is powerful. But focus also means blinkered vision, which carries dangers – but if we aren't blinkered we may be overwhelmed. Software engineers might recognize this as abstraction.

The essential characteristics of an object... the process of focusing upon the essential characteristics of an object. Grady Booch[1]

An abstraction that is appropriate for a given purpose is easier to study than the actual system because it omits details that are not relevant for that purpose. Britton, Parker and Parnas[2]

Engineers may think of OKRs as an abstraction of the desired outcome to be delivered by the end of the quarter. That outcome is described in terms that speak to the customer and the benefit to be delivered. The engineering detail, the implementation detail, are hidden behind the abstract interface.

---

[1]Grady Booch, *Object-oriented analysis and design*, 1994

[2]Kathryn Heninger Britton, R Alan Parker, David L Parnas, *A procedure for designing abstract interfaces for device interface modules*, ICSE '81: Proceedings of the 5th international conference on Software engineering, March 1981

As with software design there are different ways of approaching the same thing: each has its own benefits and tradeoffs. There may not be an obvious answer, but it is critical that everyone shares the same abstraction.

I sometimes think of OKRs as 'Test-Driven Management'. Decide what you want (the objective), next set a series of acceptance criteria: *key results*. Now get on and develop. Don't consider yourself done until you can pass the tests and meet the objectives.

When the acceptance tests are known, engineers have a wide degree of latitude in deciding how to meet their criteria. In doing so they will use their professional judgement and experience. They will also be constrained by the time and resources available: the existing products and technology will further bound a solution.

1.1 Dissecting OKRs

An objective is something you and your team wish to achieve. That objective is a goal to be achieved, something to aim for. It might be a mission in itself, or it might be part of a larger mission or some other 'higher purpose'.[3] The mission might be your product, a business initiative or some endeavour to help a client. Whatever it is, today's objective requires some significant work.

Key results are the important things that make that objective meaningful. Some like to see them as milestones, but I like to think they are more descriptive of the whole objective. Rather than describe some discrete part of the objective, I have come to see key result an attribute of the whole.

For example, an objective might be to build an electric car. 'Car can travel over 400 miles on single charge', or 'Car can be fully charged in two hours', are key results that relate the whole. It might be easier to write key results for components – 'Car has an electric engine' and 'Battery capacity exceeds 70kWh' – and the OKR is easier to achieve because those components might be individually achievable – but the ultimate objective is the whole.

Good OKRs are outcome-focused. I like to say "An objective is an outcome you wish to bring about".

OKRs are not about measuring progress towards a goal, nor are they about ticking off work items on a manifest. OKRs are about delivering outcomes that add value. That's one reason why they are a good fit with agile.

---

[3]See my earlier book *Continuous Digital* (2018) for a fuller discussion.

Each objective will have several key results. Each result should be useful in and of itself. Ideally achieving a key result should represent benefit (value). An electric car may still be useful if needs charging every 300 miles, but achieving 400 miles is worth more.

An objective should have its own *wholeness* that is more than the sum of its parts. Achieving the key results builds towards the objective, but the whole thing, the whole objective, should create more value than simply the value of the key results added together.

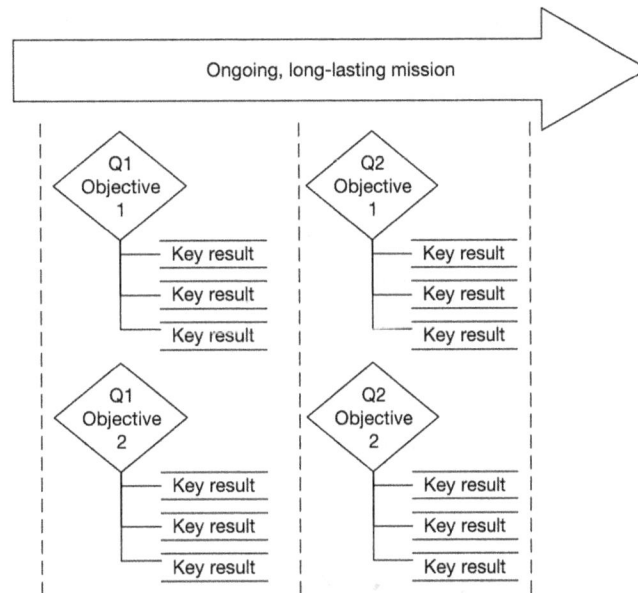

Missions are long-lasting, OKRs are reset every quarter

While missions typically last a long time, OKRs get reviewed at the end of each quarter and new ones created for the next quarter. Some may need to flow over from one quarter to another, but each OKR-setting session should start with a blank sheet. If something is worth continuing into the next quarter it's because there is more value to be gained, not because something wasn't finished or sunk costs incurred.

Teams may pursue several objectives over the course of a quarter, and each objective has several key results – hence objectives (plural) and key results (plural). But remember, the more objectives the team pursues, the less it can focus. For a really focused team it could be one objective (singular), albeit with several key results (plural).

1.2 OKRs and agile

Those schooled in agile may say "Oh, an objective is an epic, and the key results are stories", but OKRs are more than that. OKRs are not a mini-backlog, rather they are a machine for generating stories. OKRs are more akin to sprint goals; indeed each key result may be a sprint goal itself.

So throw away your epics – they aren't a perfect fit for objectives and they don't add much anyway. The objective fills the same role as an epic: *the big thing to aim at.*

Then, rather than seeing key results as stories, see them as targets. Ask yourself: *What do we need to do to move towards those targets?* Then ask again, and again. Every time you need to decide the next thing to work on, go back to the OKRs and ask the question afresh.

I'd go as far as to throw away any backlog and drive all work from the OKR story machine.

While a quarterly cycle is standard, you might choose to work on some other cycle duration. It's up to you, but working in quarters has a good rhythm.

Some see the quarterly OKR review and setting as a giant sprint. While there are similarities in the routine, the logic is different. Sprint planning is very focused on immediate action and delivering in the next few days. OKR-setting should be more thoughtful and customer (demand) focused.

Best within constraints

The aim is seldom to deliver the best-ever widget. The aim is to deliver the best possible widget within the constraints.

Constraints come in many forms. Time, people and resources are the most common, and these can usually be summed up by money. Time is always limited; the sprint and OKR cycle impose useful breakpoints. People are limited to what you have: you may get more in time, but right now you have what you have.

Solving problems within constraints is what engineers do.

1.3 Think broadly, execute narrowly

OKRs need to be measurable. While this is good because it sharpens one's thinking and enforces honesty, it is also bad because hard numbers can get in the way of big thinking. Targets can blind one to unintended consequences and side effects incurred in meeting the target; the numbers used in targets have a nasty habit of changing in unpredictable ways.

As a rule of thumb objectives are inspiring and subjective. Key results are objective and quantified with numbers.

The laser-like focus of delivering OKRs needs moderating with expansive and considered thinking during OKR-setting. Teams should alternate between reflection and broad thinking during OKR review and setting and really focused actions during delivery. The former should last hours, the latter months.

When it comes time to set OKRs again the results of the previous OKRs will inform thinking, so too should thoughts on the OKR process. Were the OKRs too vague? Too strict? Too detailed? Did enough, or too many, conversations happen beforehand?

The most perfect execution in the world is nothing if it aims for the wrong target. Equally, the most perfectly defined target is worthless if setting it uses all the time and strips away risk and motivation.

Despite the hard thinking that goes into OKR-setting, the real success of OKRs is not whether any particular objective or key result has been achieved. OKRs are *transient objects* that serve to focus thinking and work. The real benefit is in the outcomes delivered.

The ultimate objective of any OKR is to produce an outcome that creates value and benefit to customers, users and other stakeholders.

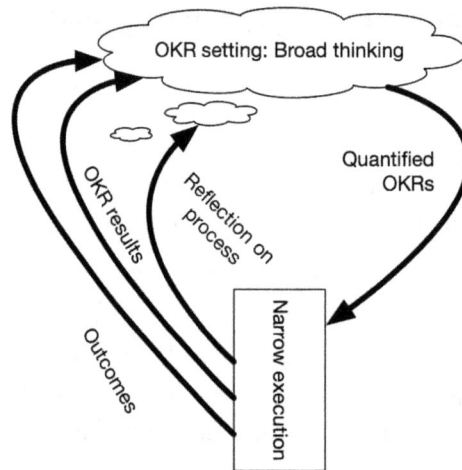

Iterate between broad thinking and narrow execution

Iterate

Think broadly for a short window of time to set OKRs.

Work narrowly for a far longer period to deliver OKRs.

Default to staying focused on OKRs during delivery, but be prepared to fight fires if need be. There is no point in delivering against targets if the world has burned down. If all you ever do is fight fires, then you will only ever be a firefighter.

1.4 Ambition over estimation

Unlike burn-down charts, velocity and story points, OKRs are not for estimation or forecasting. I'd advise against estimating any objective or key result, but rather to challenge yourself. The aim of OKRs is not to do everything, rather the aim is to be ambitious, to be prepared to push further. For that reason, OKRs shouldn't be used to benchmark teams or individuals.

Teams are not normally expected to complete 100% of their OKRs – 70% is more common. Hitting 100% is easy if the team sets easy goals. With OKRs teams are encouraged to aim high – not impossibly high, but high enough to be challenged. If teams are meeting 100% then maybe they are not aiming high enough?

Each of us want to do well and achieve 100%, in many places anything less than 100% looks like failure. Therefore it is important that leaders at all levels provide an environment in which it is safe to fail – that is, provide *psychological safety*.

Benchmarking OKRs against other teams, attaching money to OKRs, attaching blame for missed OKRs, linking performance reviews or promotion to OKRs will all destroy that safety.

Psychological safety

Psychological safety is broadly defined as a climate in which people are comfortable expressing and being themselves. More specifically, when people have psychological safety at work, they feel comfortable sharing concerns and mistakes without fear of embarrassment or retribution. They are confident that they can speak up and won't be humiliated, ignored or blamed. They know they can ask questions when they are unsure about something. They tend to trust and respect their colleagues. When a work environment has reasonably high psychological safety, good things happen: mistakes are reported quickly so that prompt corrective action can be taken; seamless coordination across groups or departments is enabled, and potentially game-changing ideas for innovation are shared. In short, psychological safety is a crucial source of value creation in organizations operating in a complex, changing environment. Amy C Edmondson, *The Fearless Organization*, 2019

When using a burn-down chart the implicit goal is to reach zero. In the traditional project model the aim is to do everything asked for, even if that needs more time. With OKRs, in contrast, achieving 100% of the targets is failure: achieving every key result and every objective suggests the team was not ambitious enough.

The thinking behind OKRs is that a team that aims high and only achieves three-quarters of their target will still deliver more benefit than a team that aims comfortably low and achieves everything. Therefore it is wrong to judge teams and individuals on how many OKRs they achieve.

Instead, when it comes to assessing performance, look at the outcome, look at the value delivered, and how things are different compared to three months ago. Ask yourself: *How is the product, the company, the world, a better place for what the team has done?*

For that reason, OKRs are not going to sit comfortably with those who want certainty. Nor are OKRs going to sit well with those who want to tell others what to do. In agile environments OKRs are likely to be set by the same people who are going to deliver them. OKRs are not about top-down control, they are more about bottom-up engagement.

Those at the top can set the final destination, give some directions and paint a picture of the promised land, but it is those who are making the journey that get to decide on the means of transport and the route. OKRs are a permission giver, not a control rod.

2. Why use OKRs?

Previously, this realization would have resulted in replanning to move out the target schedule, perhaps repeatedly. Instead, given the group's commitment to the larger result, we found a much more aggressive behaviour. For example, the OpenVMS AXP group publicly committed to their target schedule and stated, "We don't know how to achieve this, but we commit to finding a way." The next day they went to a project management consultant for training on how to build an aggressive, attainable schedule.

Peter F Conklin, director of Alpha AXP Systems Development[1]

Objectives and key results – OKRs from here on – did not start life as part of the agile toolkit. Indeed they predate 'agile' by 20 or 30 years. Yet in recent years they have received more and more attention in agile circles. More companies and teams are experimenting with them, and it's no longer uncommon to find them used by agile teams. They may not quite be a standard item in the agile toolkit, but I wouldn't be surprised if they become one.

Why? Or perhaps, what makes OKRs a good fit with agile working?

To my mind there are three reasons why OKRs work well with an agile approach: they fill a need at the mid-term planning level, OKRs are essentially a test-first approach, and OKRs enhance communication.

If OKRs sound too good to be true – and reading some authors, they *can* sound like that – then rest assured: OKRs can go wrong in many ways. The laser-like focus OKRs create needs to be tempered with countermeasures.

2.1 Mid-term planning

OKRs fill a hole in the agile planning processes that many teams struggle with. By planning, I mean planning in all its forms – software, UX and test design, coordination and scheduling.

---

[1] *Enrollment Management, Managing the Alpha AXP Program, *Digital Technical Journal* Vol. 4 No. 4 Special Issue 1992

Agile, and in particular Scrum, has plenty of short-term planning tools: the morning stand-up is a form of daily planning, Scrum and XP teams will have regular sprint/iteration planning meetings, and retrospectives are also a form of planning.

Teams usually have some long-term plan too – although these are usually independent of the chosen agile framework.

A team may have a long-term plan or a roadmap[2], a mission or vision statement, a business plan or statement of the market opportunity, maybe a *job to be done*, or a customer problem the team is addressing. Such plans usually start beyond the current quarter and may look years into the future.

However, in the middle ground lies a problem. There is no standard way of thinking about the mid-term, the period beyond the sprint but a little longer than the quarter.

Once upon a time teams created 'release plans' that showed what they planned to 'release' (or rather, build and release) during the next few weeks. For some teams that might mean sketching what would be in each of the next six release over the coming quarter (that is, three months, 13 weeks). Or it might simply be a list of what was to be included in a release that only happened once a quarter.

However with widespread adoption of continuous delivery, release plans make less sense. What is the point of a 13-week release plan when a team releases many times a day?

Other authors have suggested other solutions. I myself have advocated 'quarter plans' – that is, the plan for the coming quarter of the year[34]. I and others have tried to sketch what a process would look like around that, but since there has not been consensus on 'what is the right thing to do', few of those solutions have become mainstream.

OKRS offer the opportunity to fill that gap and provide the glue between the short-term daily and sprint planning and long-term plans.

OKRs potentially provide a way of balancing the demands of here and now with the need to steer some kind of course. By focusing on the quarter OKRs can provide mid-term goals, consistent enough over several sprints to achieve meaningful results, but flexible enough not to mislead the team.

---

[2]Roadmaps suffer from several problems themselves. All too often they are little more than a list of features with speculative dates against them.

[3]*The Art of Agile Product Ownership*, Allan Kelly, Apress, 2019

[4]*An Agile Reader*, Allan Kelly, LeanPub, 2017

> ## Quarterly, three months, 12 weeks
>
> In just about every case I have heard of, OKRs are reviewed and updated quarterly – four times a year. I can imaging using them on a shorter cycle – every six weeks maybe – or on a longer cycle, perhaps annual – but the consensus seems to be quarterly.
>
> Quarterly seems about right; three months is a good balance between thinking more strategically and getting on and doing it. It implies sticking with something for long enough to see whether it works, but not so long that one is flogging a dead horse long after it has stopped breathing.
>
> However, companies already make heavy use of quarterly cycles for things like budgets, sales targets and performance reviews. There is a good case for not adding another process on the same cadence. A ten-week or four month cadence might work better for OKR cycles. This would also avoid coupling OKRs to things like performance reviews.

2.2 Test-driven OKRs

Finally, one reason why OKRs work well with agile is that OKRs are a high-level implementation of test-driven development. I sometimes think of them as 'test-driven management'. Consequently they sit well with the agile mindset.

Each objective (the 'O') has a set of key results: the 'KRs'. Each of these key results is a test: has the result been achieved?

Each key result should be measurable. One should be able to look at the key result at the end of the period and say: did we achieve it? Or better still: how much did we achieve? How close did we get?

In other words: right at the start of the period, when setting the KRs, people are thinking "How will we know that this is done" and "How will we test that this has been achieved?"

Anyone who has practiced test-driven development at the unit test level, written acceptance criteria for a user story, or sketched a BDD-style scenario before any code is written will recognize this approach. This is what agile calls *test first*.

Test-first works well for at least two reasons. First, a test-first approach creates focus – yes, focus again! By knowing the tests that the work must pass to be successful, one is able to discount some work and measure progress towards the desired result. Anyone who has written automated test cases that show as green and red result bars will know the motivational power of such a feedback loop.

> Green means success, and you want more success!

> Red means something failed and it's damned annoying – you want to make it work!

Either way you get a dopamine hit and are motivated to carry on – fix the red thing or add more and get more green.

The second reason test-first works is because it tells you when to stop: *stop when the tests pass*.

Given any piece of work there is always a temptation to keep doing more and more – particularly when there is a positive feedback loop in place. Yet doing more and more means you will do more than is required – the famous 'gold plating' that managers believe software engineers regularly engage in.

My friends Jon Jagger and Kevlin Henney like to ask: "Why do cars have brakes?" Most people answer the question "So you can stop!" or "So you can drive safely." Jon and Kevlin like to say: "So you can drive fast."

I vividly remember the day the brakes failed on my first car. Or rather I remember driving my car to get the broken brakes fixed. The car – the engine – worked, but I had to navigate traffic lights and a hill between my apartment and the garage. As the car had manual gears (that's a stick shift for American readers), I could slow down by changing down (although I pretty much stayed in first the whole way) and use the handbrake to stop. Needless to say, I drove very, very slowly.

When you work test-first you don't stop until the tests pass[5].

That is true at the unit test level, the story level, and – with OKRs – the business objective level.

By the way, if you want a third reason why test-first works, let me add: it forces you to think about what you want in advance. While that is true, I think the first two reasons are far more powerful.

---

[5]Although when coding after the tests are passed, you probably engage in a little refactoring. Refactoring is essential, but knowing when to stop refactoring can be hard, simply because there is no test to tell you when you are done.

2.3 Communication

By summarizing the work a team has done and will do into a standardized format, OKRs make it easier to communicate what a team is doing. I like to think of OKRs as creating an interface, or API, for the team. That might be for communication within the team, with other teams, or to managers higher in the hierarchy.

Similarly, the standardized format simplifies status reporting. Today, everyone knows that 'percentage of requirements done' is a meaningless metric: teams need a way of showing what they have achieved in the current period, what they are doing now and what they (hope) to work on next. OKRs offer a way of summarizing this information.

Because OKRs offer a means of communicating status and progress, they also offer a mechanism for judging success and failure. Success motivates continuation – "More of the same please!" – while failure motivates change: "Don't let that happen again!"

A team API

The team, especially the product analysts, listen to what the senior leaders say about purpose, strategy and company objectives. They also listen to what customers and the market want. And they listen to the needs of peer teams, the product itself and many other sources of work requests.

Each cycle the team responds with OKRs which form an API - *application programming interface*. This API tells others the outcomes to expect from the team in the coming cycle. The API sets out what the team will aim to achieve, what they will forego and the priorities. There may be some negotiation during the setting process but once the OKRs are set the team is trusted to do their best.

OKRs create an API for the team

2.4 The team

In addition to communicating outside a team, OKRs enhance communication inside it. OKRs build a shared understanding and goals, and thus create a vocabulary for discussing work.

This first happens in OKR-setting, where team members have a voice about what is being proposed and how the goals are formulated. In creating focus and common goals OKRs bind the team together – more about focus in the next chapter.

Of course, such benefits depend on teams playing a role in OKR-setting. Unfortunately, where companies impose OKRs from outside the team, such benefits are lost. (Chapter 25 has more on cascading OKRs.)

2.5 Warning

Few things in life come with no downside, and OKRs carry certain risks. I'll dig into some of these risks later, but right now I want to make it clear that OKRs are not risk-free. Like any powerful tool, OKRs entail certain risks: the more you understand the risks, the better you will be at avoiding them.

Sometimes the right thing to do is throw the OKR away and work on what is in front of you. If your live server goes down and customers are without services there is no point in saying "Sorry guv'nor, I'm working on my OKR." OKRs create focus, but they shouldn't create blindness.

That philosophy extends to the results too. I'm going to argue that OKRs should be measurable, but not everything that counts can be counted. Not everything that is important can be mapped out in advance.

Consider your life partner, or, if you are single, think of your parents. When choosing to spend the rest of our lives with one person, who draws up a requirements list?

Actually, Charles Darwin did. Reportedly Darwin drew up a list of pros and cons for marriage. Cons included:

- 'Being forced to visit relatives, and to bend in every trifle'
- 'Loss of freedom to go where one liked, the conversation of clever men at clubs'
- 'Terrible loss of time'

Still Darwin concluded:

It is intolerable to think of spending one's whole life, like a neuter bee, working, working – only picture to yourself a nice soft wife on a sofa.

He ends his notes 'marry – marry – marry Q.E.D.' [6]

Darwin married Emma Wedgwood in January 1839, a little over two years after completing his journey on HMS Beagle.

Even though I, and possibly you too, like to think of ourselves as rational people when it comes to big life decisions, rational tools are often abandoned. Life partners, whether to have children or not (and how many!), divorce (Heaven forbid) and even buying a house are more likely to come down to emotion rather than rationality.

As humans we sometimes do things not because they are rational, but because we want to. Call it intuition or motivation. If we only did things that we could justify rationally (before the event) life would be boring and in time machines could probably replace us. Sometimes the important thing is *what do we want to do?*

2.6 Summary

- OKRs create focus.
- Set and reviewed on a quarterly basis, OKRs fill a gap in agile between sprints and roadmaps.
- Being test-first in nature, OKRs fit well with the agile mindset.
- Some things are more important than OKRs, and sometimes those things can't be measured.

---

[6]Darwin C, *The Autobiography of Charles Darwin*, ed. N Barlow, London, Collins, 1958 and quoted by John Kay, *Obliquity*, 2011

3. Focus

The main thing to remember is, the main thing is the main thing.

General Gary E Huffman

Focus, focus, focus.

Focus is great. I can achieve so much more when I am focused.

It is great for teams too: much of my work involves creating team focus – making sure everyone on the team is aiming at the same thing, addressing the same problems and working in a similar fashion.

Focus only happens when you have partial blindness: as with a camera lens, focusing on one thing means not focusing on others – it means some things move out of vision. Of course that is dangerous, but *how is one to focus if one is constantly looking at everything?*

The trick is to move consciously between the two states. Carve out time to be focused, but allow time to think more broadly.

3.1 OKRs create focus

A lot of commentators writing about OKRs emphasize the aspirational nature of OKRs and their ability to inspire a team to 'do great'. Personally I see the aspirational nature of teams more as a function of company culture: companies with a culture of reaching for the stars will use OKRs to reach for the stars. Companies with more work-a-day cultures will use OKRs differently.

For me the key thing about OKRs is the ability to focus minds. The three-month OKR cycle resembles a long sprint and the OKRs a story-generating machine. That is not to say that OKRs are an excuse for three-month sprints, rather they are the overarching guide for the sprints in the quarter.

Focus is so often the secret ingredient that makes things happen. I suspect everyone has a mental list of things they should do. I know many people like me have an actual list of things *to do* sometime in the near future. But I also know that such intentions and plans are easily blown off course by – well – life.

Unexpected things have a bad habit of happening in the work environment: customer issues appear and get in the way of the work you plan to do; the only calendar slot for the really important meeting is next month, not next week; technology doesn't work the way you think it will and work takes days rather than hours; the coffee machine stops working and you lose your liquid energy and waste time trying to make it work.

And that's before one considers the human and social side: trains run late, children get ill and need attention, boilers break down and you need to stay at home for the technician, companies have Christmas parties – the list could go on and on.

When you attain focus you can do amazing stuff. Better still, when your whole team can focus on the same thing at the same time, things can really move.

One can hope to achieve focus, one can even plan for focus – I do so most mornings – but it is so easy to lose focus and get blown off course by trivia. It helps to stay on course if one has a reason to say "No" – or at least say "Can it wait?".

To my mind the biggest single reason for using OKRs is that they help to improve focus – not just the focus of individuals, but the collective focus of a team.

Many of the tools in the standard agile toolkit also create focus: daily stand-up meetings create focus for the day, planning meetings create focus for the sprint, visual boards highlight work in progress and focus attention on moving it to 'done', acceptance criteria focus work on a story and more. OKRs also have the power to create focus.

All these tools give us an opportunity and a reason to say "No" to work that detracts from focus. Because OKRs are bigger, because OKRs may be approved by more senior people, because OKRs are important and involve other people, then OKRs provide more leverage to say "No, I can't do that right now".

That is not to say that one should refuse all requests that do not align with an OKR: there are times when it makes sense to put the OKR to one side in favour of something else. I'll discuss these scenarios later; for the moment, let's just say that OKRs help bring focus.

Digital distractions

As useful as our digital devices – phones, tablets, watches and such – are, I can't help but wonder if the constant stream of notifications and demands on our time make focus even more difficult to achieve.

It is not so much the devices themselves as the social networks that inhabit them: Facebook, LinkedIn, Instagram and, worst of all, Twitter – and I used to struggle with Twitter addiction. I almost feel sorry for employers who must compete for employees attention!

In a world where advertisers and social networks so often win our time and attention, achieving purposeful focus becomes more valuable. The less focus there is in the world, the greater the benefits for those who can achieve purposeful focus.

3.2 Summary

- OKRs are great at creating team focus – both agreeing what to focus on, then delivering against that focus.

4. OKR history

No organization which purposefully and systematically abandons the unproductive and obsolete ever wants for opportunities...

The normal human reaction is to evade the priority decision by doing a little bit of everything.

Peter Drucker, *Age of Discontinuity*, 1992

Once upon a time there was a management guru called Peter Drucker. He advocated 'management by objective' – or MBO[1]. The idea was for managers to decide strategic objectives that the organization would pursue; effort and resources are then directed to meet these objectives.

Drucker was not the first to advocate MBOs and he was not the last. Differences exist in how writers describe the use of MBOs and how companies implement them.

In general, MBOs are interpreted as a top-down mechanism: senior managers decree the MBOs, middle managers instruct their department to undertake the MBOs. The workers at the end of the process are but recipients.

Andy Grove[2] invented OKRs in the early days of Intel Corporation. At the time Grove was a senior manager at Intel; he went on to become company CEO. Grove saw delivery as key: in devising OKRs he extended MBOs with a focus on delivery.

As one of the earliest and most successful Silicon Valley companies, Intel's approach permeated Silicon Valley culture and many of the start-ups that followed. Intel alumni carried OKRs to new companies, and given Intel's success, many were only too happy to copy.

Success bred success: the more people heard of OKRs, the more companies tried using them. The more companies that succeeded using OKRs, the more other companies wanted to copy them. That does not mean they were universally adopted in Silicon Valley, but they did become common.

---

[1] *The Practice of Management*, Peter Drucker, 1954
[2] *Measure what Matters*, John Doerr, 2018

One particular ex-Intel engineer became prominent in spreading OKRs: John Doerr. After leaving Intel Doerr became a successful venture capital investor. In this role he held an influential position with many start-ups and advocated the use of OKRs.

In 1999 Doerr invested in the company that was to eclipse all his other investments: Google. Next Doerr introduced OKRs, Google's founders and early employees were eager adopters and – as they say – the rest is history.

Interest in OKRs continued to grow, and news of their success at Google further increased their allure. In 2018 Doerr published *Measure what Matters* in which he tells stories from Intel, Google and elsewhere while explaining OKRs in more detail.

1999 was also the year that Extreme Programming[3] burst onto the scene. XP was one of several 'lightweight development methods' that were rebranded as 'agile' in 2001. It was only a matter of time before companies started to use both agile and OKRs.

While MBOs are still in widespread use, they have fallen out of fashion in many quarters. Experience with MBOs has shown several problems. Doerr suggests that in their formulation and use, OKRs rectify such problems.

Doerr's comparison of MBOs and OKRs

MBOs	Intel OKRs
'What'	'What' and 'How'
Annual	Quarterly or monthly
Private and siloed	Public and transparent
Top-down	Bottom-up or sideways (∼50%)
Tied to compensation	Mostly divorced from compensation
Risk-averse	Aggressive and aspirational

One should not pretend that the OKRs mechanism is without issues. Later chapters discuss some problems and issues you should be aware of. Like a sharp sword, OKRs can be amazingly useful, but they also need to be handled carefully, lest they harm their users.

---

[3]*Extreme Programming Explained,* Kent Beck, 2000

5. Outcomes, value and benefits

Value is perceived benefit: that is, the benefit we think we will get from something.

Tom Gilb, *Concept 269, Competitive Engineering*, 2007

OKRs aim to achieve some objective – *the 'O'*. That objective should be an outcome – something that has been changed, something that has been achieved, something that makes the world – or at least one person – happier. Strive for *outcomes over outputs*, little bits of change over more stuff.

Outcomes should be things in their own right and not proxies for something else. For example, counting work 'done' on a tracking chart – be it a project plan or burn-down – is a proxy measurement for the work itself. However, outcomes can be subjective: one person's outcome is another person's milestone.

Outcomes are often wrapped inside other outcomes. The thing *you* define as an outcome of your work might be little more than a milestone or proxy measurement along the route to an outcome *I* am aiming for.

Not all outcomes are equal, some have more validity than others. The term 'vanity metrics' describes quantified measurements that don't actually represent a beneficial outcome.

By temperament, training or sheer desperation, people often value the proxy instead of the actual outcome. Consider a large initiative to build a new online shopping platform. Some may see feature completion as a useful outcome, but others may argue that nothing is complete until it is in use by actual customers.

When defining objectives, always strive for outcomes rather than proxies. Be prepared to challenge yourself and let others challenge you. Know the people your outcome will benefit: preferably be able to name them. Seek to remove any intermediaries between your outcome and actual end customers receiving benefit.

It might be impossible to define perfect customer-enhancing outcomes; some element of proxy might remain. Just be prepared to challenge easy answers and go as far as you can.

Remember that money itself is a feedback mechanism: when customers part with cold hard cash in return for your outcome it is a form of feedback. A customer paying $100 for your product indicates that the customer is prepared to give up the other things that $100 could have provided.

5.1 Business benefit and value

Outcomes should benefit customers, the wider business and even society itself. Although it is easy to talk about businesses as monolithic blobs, all organizational entities are collections of people. Ultimately benefits flow to individual people.

Maybe an outcome makes someone's job easier, more productive, more satisfying or just more fun to do. Sometimes the benefits accrue to managers who are responsible for a process, product or group of employees.

An outcome may create benefits for an external customer: maybe the outcome is a better product, a cheaper product, a more widely available product or one of many other benefits.

In addition to internal users and external customers, there are plenty of other stakeholders: shareholders, regulators, customers-of-customers, special interest groups (think Greenpeace or the WWF), the families of employees and more.

In general, the words 'value' and 'benefit' are synonymous. Value has the advantage that it is slightly shorter, but the disadvantage that people tend to associate 'value' with a number. Benefit fits more easily when talking about non-financial value.

Business

When I use the word 'business' I mean it in a very broad sense. 'Business' includes commercial 'profit maximizing' companies and more.

Government entities are businesses too: the IRS is in the business of collecting US taxes, the British NHS is in the business of healthcare and the Bangkok Metropolitan Administration is in the business of providing local government.

Charities and other 'third sector' entities are included too, whether they be local, national or international – the Red Cross is in the business of protecting human life and health, Greenpeace is in the business of ensuring *the ability of the Earth to nurture life in all its diversity.*

With a commercial enterprise, it easy to equate benefit and value with money, the value added to the bottom line or increased profit. For non-commercial entities one has to look harder and ask: "What does this business value?". In truth, asking the same of commercial enterprises holds great value itself; not everything of value appears in company accounts.

5.2 Value

Value may come in different forms. Money is a perhaps the most obvious form of value, but it is not the only one.

Learning is valuable, for example gaining knowledge of new technologies or learning better ways to create the product. Learning also happens as you understand your customers more, how they use the product and the problems they face.

Feedback is valuable, as it feeds learning and helps extend our existing knowledge. Perhaps the most valuable form of feedback is that which doesn't fit our existing models and understanding. Such feedback often looks like failure but can be the most valuable, because it forces us to relearn.

Feedback is valuable in itself and helps create value. Perhaps feedback allows for price increases or cost reductions.

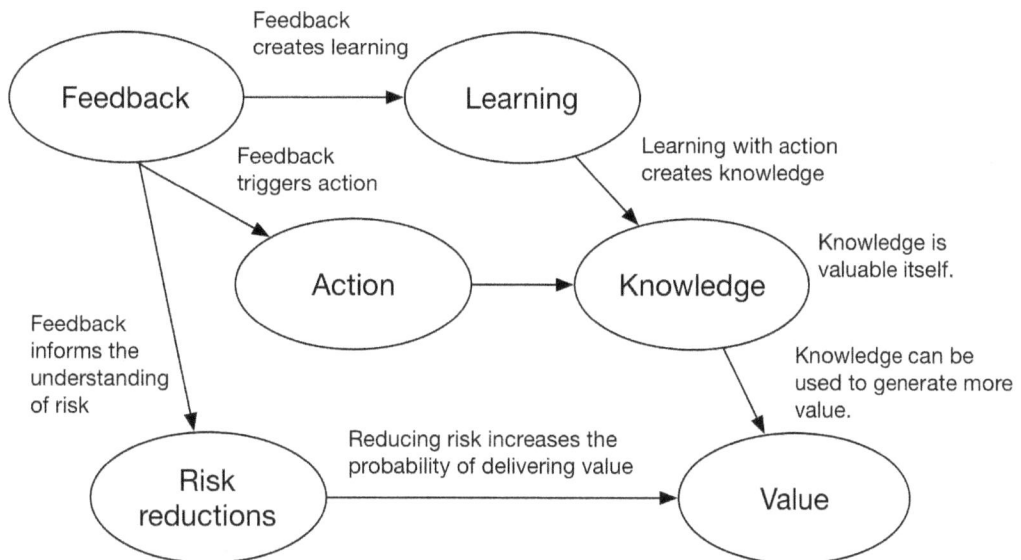

Feedback creates value in multiple ways

Risk reduction is valuable: there is always some uncertainty attached to an outcome, so reducing risk increases the likelihood of achieving the outcome and the value.

Risk reduction is valuable, but risk reduction costs. Economists like to say that 'profit is the reward for risk'. The cost of removing all risk may be negation of all benefit. For example, delaying the start of work by one month may reduce risk, so is valuable, but a later start means a later end which, thanks to cost-of-delay, may mean that the value lost is greater than the value gained.

Money: while not the only form of value, do not overlook simple money. In a modern free-market economy incoming revenue is not only necessary to pay our salaries: income also tells us what other people (our customers) value. I like to joke that "Money is the best form of feedback".

Similarly, money saved (costs reduced) tells us that there is a more efficient way to do the same thing. Saving money in one place frees money for use elsewhere, which allows businesses to adapt and change.

Even when outcomes deliver money, subjectivity is still at work. Accounting techniques (such as exceptional items and capital expenditure) provide for a lot of judgement calls. To complicate things further, the 'financial engineering' performed by corporate financiers and bankers can produce a reality distortion field.

Ultimately value is recognized by people. As a general rule the more people who value an outcome, the more valuable it is.

5.3 Pieconomics

In *Grow the Pie*, business school professor Alex Edmans[1] calls for a broad interpretation of value. Edmans argues that by taking a board-level 'stakeholder value' approach to value rather than a narrow 'shareholder value' view, companies can increase the total value they generate both for shareholders and for society.

To Edmans the value created is a pie – hence *pieconomics*. For one group to receive more there are two options: either they can take more of the same pie for themselves, thereby leaving others with less, or they can grow the pie so that there is more for all. Edmans argues that too often commercial enterprises merely resize the slices when they could make more value for all by growing the overall pie.

Perhaps the first job for any leader is to clearly say whether they are leading a pie-growing or pie-splitting endeavour.

Edmans recognizes that value is not always monetary and doesn't always appear on a balance sheet. Organizations create value not just for shareholders, but also for customers, employees and others in society. Such value may not be financial. Thus, simply chasing financial targets ignores other ways in which value is created for society.

---

[1]*Grow the Pie*, Alex Edmans, 2020

Importantly, he points out that even in financial terms it can be impractical or even impossible to calculate the return on many decisions. He discusses, for example, how Apple could calculate the financial return on building an employee gym, but he concludes that while theoretically possible, such a calculation is both impractical and would always be inaccurate. The decision to build or not to build a gym is down to judgement rooted in Apple's values.

Organizations that understand their higher purpose, which have a sense of mission and understand their role and obligations as part of society, can generate value in many forms.

This is not to argue that companies should ignore profit. Edmans presents compelling evidence that pursing a larger pie for all, creating non-financial value and benefitting society, actually brings superior financial rewards too. There is no need to choose between more value for the few and the many.

Estimate value

In *A Little Book of Requirements and User Stories* I describe how to estimate value – that is, to put a number on the value of a user story. I argue that estimation should use an abstract 'business points' currency akin to 'story points'. I advise against trying to estimate in a real currency such as dollars or euros.

Importantly, this approach generates good conversations about what is valuable, why it is valuable and even *what value is*. Value estimation is applicable to OKRs too, and because individual estimators are free to consider and argue for factors they consider important, non-financial stakeholder value get included too.

5.4 Summary

- OKRs aim to deliver outcomes that create value and deliver benefit to stakeholders both within and outside the organization.
- Value comes in many different forms and accrues directly and indirectly to customers, shareholders and the wider society.
- Money and numbers present a way of quantifying value, but they are not the only measures of value.
- Aiming to grow the pie for all not only benefits society, but is also likely to lead to higher profits.

II Writing OKRs

Determine that the thing can and shall be done, and then we shall find the way.

A goal properly set is halfway reached.

Abraham Lincoln, 1809–1865, President of the United States

6. Writing OKRs

"Less is more"

"God is in the details"

Ludwig Mies van der Rohe, architect, 1886–1969

Quarterly writing of new OKRs is primarily a strategy question: *what are the strategic priorities for the next quarter?* It requires broad thinking. What does the team aim to do? What targets will the team set for itself? More importantly: what will the team not do?

Delivering those goals is an operational issue. It demands narrow, focused, action – prioritization. Think strategically when setting, think narrowly when delivering.

Prioritization is not just about deciding what to do, it is also about deciding what not to do. In writing OKRs for the coming quarter a team is consciously deciding what it will aim for. Perhaps more importantly, the team is also saying what it will not aim for. Everything that is not in the OKRs is, by definition, lower priority.

If one is totally honest, for many – if not most – teams, if something is not in the OKRs for a quarter it stands little if any chance of being done. Teams are expected to give OKRs the best shot possible. Doing work that does not support an OKR displaces work that does.

This can be a hard pill to swallow, but experience shows that it is immensely powerful. It is a lesson that is learned over and over again. Whether it be Peter Drucker, agile or OKRs, the message is the same: prioritize, focus, execute. This author relearns the same lesson several times a year.

Blinkered servitude to goals can be as damaging as the randomness of no goals and no shared aims. OKRs mitigate this danger by involving team members in setting goals and by reviewing and resetting goals on a regular basis, normally quarterly.

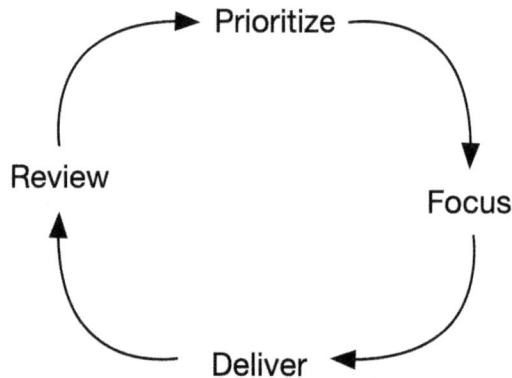

OKRs operate within a cycle: prioritize, focus, deliver and review

The following chapters discuss the objective and key results part of OKRs individually. First, though, some ground rules.

6.1 Team setting

OKRs that are handed down from above for a team to deliver run against the self-organizing ethos of agile: one cannot impose ambition on team members. The OKR-setting process is an opportunity to enrol team members in the objectives.

In an agile environment team members, including you and me, expect to have a voice in setting team OKRs. Some team members, for example a Product Owner or team leader, may have a privileged position in setting OKRs, but they do not have a free hand.

Yet involving all team members as near-equals may create another problem, one that economists call *satisficing*. This occurs when people aim to 'play it safe' and avoid risk – team members agree to set goals that they feel can be achieved comfortably.

Before engaging in OKR-setting the team should clarify where they stand on the aspiration spectrum: *are you setting utility OKRs or aspirational OKRs?*

'Utility OKRs' serve to prioritize, organize and communicate work. They do not embody aspirations – teams may deliberately seek to stay in their comfort zone. Utility OKRs go against a lot of OKR literature that emphasizes aspirations. But organizations that value predictability or lack psychological safety such OKRs can still be useful, and may be a stepping stone towards more aspiration.

Also be clear what the organization and related teams expect of you. While organizations may expect aspirational OKRs, teams may shy away from ambition and *play it safe*.

To complicate matters, other teams may not agree. While one team may embrace ambition and aim high (while knowing they may fall short), other teams may value predictability and set goals they are confident can be achieved without stretching. This causes tension, especially when such teams need to work together.

I remember being in one meeting in which my team presented their OKRs for the quarter. An internal customer asked "How many of these OKR do you expect to achieve?". I said I didn't know for sure, but 70% would be reasonable. The other team reacted with horror. Their team valued predictability: 70% was 30% too short.

Mark aspirations

Some teams mark objectives or key results that they feel to be aspirational. For example, an asterisk is placed on those that they feel are more stretching.

When delivery of particular goals are required by specific dates, teams could adopt a similar strategy. These could be marked with, say, a dollar symbol '$', to indicate value in predictable delivery. This could even be followed by a particularly important date, for example 'Android port working $July23'.

However, the greater the aspirational outcomes a team aims for, the less likely it is that they will be achieved. Similarly, the more defined deadline items there are, the more likely it becomes that aspirations will be missed.

The odd aspirational or fixed deadline item in a team's OKRs probably isn't an issue. Having a lot, though, could be a sign that the team is losing its autonomy and external stakeholders are trying to control it.

6.2 Limited number

The aim of the OKRs is to create focus, so it is self-defeating to set too many OKRs. If you have 20 OKRs, which do you focus on? Of course if the OKRs are set at the team level, and there are 20 people on the team, each could have their own OKR. But is that really focus? Is it even agile?

Teams exist to share work – multi-skilled and cross functional – towards a common purpose, especially in an agile environment. OKRs serve to provide that purpose, so it makes sense to have OKRs that allow the team to focus collectively.

So how many OKRs? That depends on how tightly you want to focus and how many things are being demanded of the team. OKRs serve to help say "No" – or at least "Not now".

Personally I've come to the conclusion that three is the maximum. While I'd like it to be fewer, two or even one, I more often find myself going in the other direction and accepting four. For the teams I've worked with four seems to work. Or rather, I try and hold the line at three, but accept four. Possibly if I tried to draw the line at four I'd end up having to accept five.

So if you want a hard answer to the question "How many OKRs should a team set?", the answer is 'Three... OK, maybe four.'

This rule of thumb serves both for the number of objectives and the number of key results for each objective. So aim for a maximum of three objectives, or four if you must, each of which has a maximum of three (or four if you really need them) key results. That is now nine (3x3) and 16 (4x4) results to aim for.

In my book 16 is a lot: even nine risks losing focus. A quarterly OKR cycle is 13 weeks, so this equates with slightly more than one week per key result to slightly less than one key result a week. Either way that is not a lot of time; those key results can't be too ambitious. If you want more ambition you probably need fewer key results on which to focus. But before you say "But doesn't it depend on team size?", let me say: no.

Certainly a larger team can do more stuff, but that dilutes focus. The aim of OKRs is to achieve collective focus and goals: the more things you try and focus on, the less sharp the focus will be. Too many results ends up looking like a shopping list of things to do.

Paradoxically, bigger teams should aim for fewer OKRs. When teams are bigger it is harder to achieve focus. Bigger teams do not deliver more OKRs, bigger teams demand more focus. Rather than load a big team with six OKRs, I would prefer to split the team in two and ask each to pursue a few OKRs.

Remember, in limiting the number you are not claiming that all the other things are worthless and we won't do them. What you are saying is "All these things are worth doing, but if we try to do them all we won't get very far with any of them. So we will accept a few, and do our damnedest to get them done, and then we will look again." In other words, right now, of all the things you *could* do, you need to just select a few to focus on.

6.3 Priority

So you set three (or four) OKRs.

That does not mean all OKRs are equal: some might be higher priority than others. Since when written down the OKRs will form a sequence – and may even be numbered – it is natural to see the one at the top as the highest priority, the one to do first.

In the spirit of 'do the simplest thing that could possibly work', it makes eminent sense to order the OKRs in priority order. The one at the top of the list is highest priority, and the one at the bottom lowest.

There are those who might insist that all OKRs are equal. This runs counter to the philosophy of 'prioritize, focus and execute'. Prioritization may be a hard decision, but it has a large payoff because it promotes focus, and focus promotes execution.

Before you accept that two OKRs are genuinely both priority one, ask "Is it better to achieve one completely and progress the other, or is it better to advance both but complete neither?". If the latter is true then maybe the OKRs – or at least the key results – need to be broken down a little.

While it complicates things, it is possible to prioritize key results independently of objectives by interleaving them. For example: key result #1 of objective #1, key result #1 of objective #2, result #2 and #3 of objective #1, remaining objective #2 key results... But I'd rather you didn't do it like this, simply because it complicates matters – although it is possible.

6.4 Effort

In an ideal world a team would have but one objective and could systematically work through key results. More often teams find that each objective could absorb all the time available, but the team needs to make progress against multiple objectives.

In such cases it makes sense to allocate effort against OKRs. For example, suppose you have a team of five people and you are going to be working on delivering three OKRs for the next 12 weeks (six sprints). You therefore have 60 days. You might want to allocate effort as follows:

- OKR 1: 10 days
- OKR 2: 40 days
- OKR 3: 10 days

Or if you are running two-week sprints:

- OKR 1: one sprint
- OKR 2: four sprints
- OKR 3: one sprint

Notice here that priority does not correspond to the capacity allocated. It is entirely possible to say "OKR 1 is our highest priority, we really need to make progress here, but it does not need to absorb lots of time." It is important to recognize that priority and capacity allocation are different things: just because something is important does not mean it should take up a lot of time.

This is a rudimentary form of *capacity planning*. There are three keys to making this work:

1. Teams have to stop at the end of the time: they cannot say "We used all ten days, but haven't finished and need more time." They need to have something deliverable at the end of the time-box.
2. The team will not produce the perfect solution, or even a complete solution: the team will aim to improve the current position – that is, the outcome will be better than the status quo.
3. The team has the authority (and skills) to decide what to do: it is given an objective and trusted to move toward the objective.

For example, suppose you've been asked to tender for some work for a new client. It might be really important to spend some time writing the proposal, but that does not mean it should absorb lots of time.

Importantly: capacity allocations are not estimates.

To produce estimates requires some pre-work. At the very least it requires someone to sit down and think about the work and think of some number, an 'estimate'. That in turn means that someone, the same person or someone else, needs to specify what the work is – what used to be called 'requirements'. That may lead to a discussion of 'designing' the thing. Suddenly there is a lot of pre-work to do and a lot of assumptions are being made.

While well-intentioned, pre-work creates problems.

> ## Working backwards
>
> If you follow my advice you will have three or four objectives each with three or four key results. That is between nine and 16 key results in total – and 16 sounds too many – so say about 12 on average.
>
> Assume OKRs are set quarterly (that is, 13 weeks) – less one week for reviewing and setting OKRs. So each key result has one week of total team time. That's not a lot.
>
> While you probably won't execute each key result in sequence, this simple calculation gives you some idea of how much work should be involved in a single key result and how fast you should be ticking them off as the weeks go by.

6.5 Avoid planning by OKR

Teams can be tempted to use OKRs to explain their plan of action. To use an example taken from Itamar Gilad[1]:

> 'Objective: become a leader in the enterprise
>
> Key result: launch v2.2 of the mobile app
>
> Key result: integrate with sales force
>
> Key result: switch to new onboarding flow
>
> Key result: run ten paid campaigns'

As Gilad says:

> 'Here's why this is wrong. Objectives and key results are designed to convey goals — what we're trying to achieve, by when and how we'll measure success. Building, launching and promoting features and products are not the goals. The goals are the benefits we expect to gain from these actions.'

---

[1] *5 Ways Your Company May Be Misusing OKRs*, Itamar Gilad, https://itamargilad.com/5-ways-your-company-may-be-misusing-okrs/, access July 2020

This demonstrates another problem with OKRs as plans: the dependency problem. If key result 1 is missed, then the following key results will also be missed – a domino effect. While it is sometimes impossible to avoid one key result depending on an earlier one, it is obviously better if they are independent. Such dependencies create fragility and hinder agility. (Later chapters return to this problem.)

6.6 The trouble with pre-work

Plans codified as OKRs suggests that some pre-work has been done to create a plan to start with. While pre-work itself is not inherently bad, it does imply that someone is spending time undertaking the pre-work. Such pre-work is by definition not part of the current quarter's OKRs: focus, time and effort are being diverted from the current OKRs. Thus pre-work makes hitting the current objectives harder.

Every day that an architect spends thinking about work that they expect to happen next quarter is a day not spent doing the work of this quarter. Plus, pre-work may be completely wasted if the objective changes or gets pushed back.

However there is a more insidious problem here. While performing pre-work may appear rational and conscientious, it can be self-limiting. Looking at the work in advance may discourage people from taking on ambitious work or deliberately reducing the goal.

Then there is the problem with effort estimates, which are notorious for being wrong. What if your analysis and estimates indicate that the work will take more than the quarter? Should you reduce the target? To do so would be to reduce your ambition.

What if your analysis suggests that the OKR will fit into this quarter, but only just. Does that make it too risky to take on? Should you allow contingency? What if the contingency takes the OKR beyond the quarter? Does that mean that another objective is squeezed out of this quarter?

As well as reducing your capacity in this quarter, pre-work may lead you to be less aspirational.

6.7 When to set OKRs

OKRs should be set collectively by the team, in a timely manner and with thought. Setting OKRs too early is problematic, because things change and the OKR-setting process is a distraction from current work. Setting OKRs too late is also problematic, because they don't get the consideration they deserve.

There is no specific time to set OKRs. When they are set will depend on the corporate calendar, your chosen OKR cadence, how many other teams and stakeholders you need to consult with, whether anyone is doing longer-term planning (see later chapters) and when the team has time.

However OKRs should not be set weeks and weeks in advance of the quarter for which they will apply. Nor should they be set at the last minute: teams need time to discuss the objectives.

A few weeks in advance, say two or three, should be fine. Let them marinate for a few days and then review them. I've come to believe the last week of the quarter should be used to close current OKRs and set new ones. That might make for a busy week, but that is what I will aim for next time.

6.8 Not money

Visionary companies pursue a cluster of objectives, of which making money is only one – and not necessarily the primary one. Yes, they seek profits, but they're equally guided by a core ideology – core values and sense of purpose beyond just making money. Yet paradoxically, the visionary companies make more money than the purely profit-driven companies. Jim Collins and Jerry Porras, *Built to Last*, 1994

For a commercial enterprise all goals might ultimately be reduced to 'Make more money'. Don't do this.

Those who read business books such as *Built to Last* will notice a common theme: *the power of purpose*. Management guru after management guru advocate for businesses to have a purpose above and beyond making money. Earning money, making profits, is simply a side effect of fulfilling a company's purpose.

As Alex Edmunds, who I discussed in Chapter 5, puts it in *Grow the Pie*: "The pie-growing mentality... aspires to grow the pie – to create value for society – because doing so benefits both investors and stakeholders alike. Profits, then, are no longer the end goal, but instead arise as a byproduct of creating value".

Conversely, few business books or management gurus actually argue for the pursuit of revenue and profit as an end in themselves. There is a reason for this – *money doesn't motivate people.* Few people, and even fewer software engineers, find making money motivating. Some are, certainly – some people want to make lots of money, and that's fine. But few people get out of bed in the morning thinking "Yippee, today I'm going to make more money for the company".

OKRs need to represent value, and value might mean money, but there needs to be more meaning to the objective than simply bringing in more money. Profit is a side effect of delivering on that purpose and creating value.

> *The profit seeking paradox... the most profitable companies are not the most profit-oriented.* John Kay, *Obliquity*, 2011

6.9 Summary

- Think strategically when setting OKRs, prioritize and don't try to do everything.
- agile ethos OKRs demand that the teams who will deliver them set them.
- OKRs should be aspirational, although aspirations may need to be tempered for the environment.
- Creating focus with OKRs demands that the number of OKRs for each cycle is limited to no more than most people can count on the fingers of one hand.
- The length and events of the OKR cycle, the amount of pre-planning and estimation, differ between teams.
- OKR outcomes should deliver value, but that does not mean targeting money directly.

7. Objectives

Objectives within objectives – like Russian Matryoska dolls

In the process of decision those alternatives are chosen which are considered to be appropriate means of reaching desired ends. Ends themselves, however, are often merely instrumental to more final objectives. We are thus led to the conception of a series, or hierarchy, of ends.

Herbert A Simon, *Administrative Behavior*, 1947

So the first thing to decide is: *what is the objective?* or, to put it another way, *what is the outcome you are seeking?*

Key results help to define and build towards that objective, so the first thing to write is the objective. The objective needs to be something the organization wants, something the organization values, something that contributes towards the bigger goals and visions that leaders have outlined.

The objective is the thing you are trying to achieve, perhaps the thing you are trying to build or create, or perhaps a change you are seeking to make. Your objective may be only a part of someone else's grand plan, a building block on the way to another objective: that in turn might be a small part of something bigger.

The objective does not so much describe the problem you are trying to solve. Rather, the objective is the state in which the solution has been build and the problem has been resolved.

Although I write 'problem', I could just as easily write 'opportunity'. It may not seem it at the time, but problems can be opportunities in disguise. In which case, the objective is the state in which the opportunity has been seized.

The objective doesn't need to explain the problem in detail, or how you know it is a problem. Rather, it is the objective that is the resolution of the problem or realization of the opportunity.

Objectives should inspire, so don't let details get in the way. This also means objectives are often free of quantification. The place for numbers is in the key results. At the risk of abusing the English language, one might say "Objectives are subjective, key results are objective".

7.1 Background analysis

You may want to do some analysis to make sure you are addressing the right problem with your objective. You might even want to share your analysis and reasoning with others. However, the OKR itself is not the place to do this. The objective should be short and sweet.

If you need to explain your choice of analysis and reasoning then do so: sometimes explaining oneself can provide new insights – but don't include that explanation in the OKRs. Park the rationale, the explanation, elsewhere. Your objective can always be accompanied by a footnote that tells the reader where to find out why that objective was chosen.

In my experience, as long as the objective has value and someone can verbally explain why the objective was chosen, then little or no supporting collateral is needed.

7.2 Objective value

It goes without saying that the objective should be meaningful and deliver some benefit to the organization. If the objective does not deliver business benefit of some form, why pursue it?

'Business benefit' is a bit of a mouthful – seven vowels – so it is easier to talk about *value* – does the objective have value?

That's fine, except that to many ears 'value' implies a number, and a number implies a financial quantity, maybe $100,000 or €1,000,000. In a commercial enterprise it is wonderful when an objective results in hard cash, but not all objectives deliver money, and money is not the only measure of value.

A previous chapter discussed value, so just note that valuable outcomes can include:

- Learning: by the team ("We learnt Scala this quarter") or by the business ("We learned that our customers prefer green").
- Risk reduction: for the piece of work the team is focused on or for the wider organization.
- Strategy advancement: executing on strategy goals may mean incurring costs and risks today that will not pay back for a long time.
- Furthering the aims of stakeholders and society at large.

Money, such as new revenue or cost savings, can also be an outcome. Remember that despite what is often claimed, few people are really motivated by money.

Note too that I'm avoiding the term 'profit'. That's for two reasons. Firstly, profit is constructed by accountants. There are so many rules regarding what is profit and what is not that it becomes a subjective thing. Private equity companies in particular have a habit of loading companies with debt that wipes out any profit but in doing so reduces tax. The net effect is that the private equity company makes a bigger return.

The second reason for avoiding profit is that stating an objective as 'Make more profit' is so general as to be meaningless. Such an objective doesn't really say much about what the objective actually is.

7.3 Obvious value

When crafting an objective, make the value the objective brings blindingly obvious. That the usefulness of the objective is obvious to you, and even to your team, does not mean that it is obvious to others. Don't worry about 'dumbing down' – wait until people tell you that you are stating the obvious before you start making assumptions.

In particular, it may not be obvious to your senior managers. So...

Retool the delivery pipeline to facilitate continuous delivery.

Might be better phrased as:

> Accelerate time to market by retooling the delivery pipeline to adopt continuous delivery approaches.

Which could be still better stated as:

> Increase return on investment by reducing time to market with a new delivery pipeline and continuous delivery practices.

Hopefully you can see a way to spell out the value even more clearly.

The old user story technique of appending a 'so that' to the end of an objective can help here:

> Reduce the time it takes to complete regression testing.

Becomes:

> Reduce the time it takes to complete regression testing *so that* time to market is reduced and the cost of testing is reduced.

Although the problem with 'so that' is that it comes at the end. Therefore bring the benefit to the front:

> Reduce time to market and testing effort by reducing time spent in regression testing.

These become like Matryoska dolls: you can continue refining and improving objectives almost infinitely. However there comes a point of diminishing returns, where an extra 20 minutes spent on the next improvement won't make much difference. Far better to take a break, come back a day or two later and look at them with fresh eyes.

Better still, try them out one someone else.

7.4 Wide objectives

The objective part of an OKR is the place to 'go wide'. What you want is a beneficial outcome. You want to avoid boxing yourself into a specific approach or solution – you might do that in the key results – but leave yourself space in the objective. That space allows the team to make tradeoffs so as to find a solution within the constraints of technology and time. When the objective is so specific that it allows for only one solution, tradeoffs are not possible and options are closed. Consequently the team is disempowered and the chances of achieving the objectives diminished.

What you want is an outcome statement that has clear business value but which is wide enough for the delivery team to be able to find different ways of realizing that objective. For example:

> Show competitive advantage in data processing by ingesting priority data sources faster than competitor XYZ.

Faced with this objective, the delivery team may start by profiling the application and finding where it spends its time, then methodically working through each to increase speed. While rational, this approach might itself be time-consuming.

Alternatively, the team might use its existing knowledge and make an educated guess as to which part of the application requires attention. This might be a database change, or it might be application logic rework.

Another approach might be to improve the data connection between the application server and the main data sources. This might even mean physically moving resources from one data centre to another. In the extreme it might mean paying extra to locate machines next to one another.

Given three ways of meeting their goal, the team might decide to pursue all three in parallel – a set-based engineering approach[1]. The team might pursue all three options to their conclusion, or reduce the number when one option shows that it can deliver the expected result.

It can be helpful to ask the team *how might we approach this?* when setting the objective. In answering the question don't try to find one complete answer, seek to find several probably feasible options.

---

[1]Morgan and Liker, *The Toyota Product Development System*, 2006

Sometimes something that looks narrowing may actually widen the options. Look at the word 'priority' in the previous example. Including that word in the objective may look as if the objective is narrowed, but it actually allows more scope for creative approaches.

In this case the team has the scope to focus just on the priority sources. General changes are not required. The team could reprogram the application to simply prioritize a limited number of data sources – the priority ones.

Writing objectives that allow for different approaches lets the team doing the work decide the best way to deliver an outcome within the constraints they face on the day.

> Tom Gilb tells a story of an attempt by the US Army to rewrite their logistics system in the 1990s. This multi-year effort was cut short when the army realized the real need was not for everyone to have a faster system, but for *generals* to have a faster system. Changing the existing logistics system to prioritize by the rank of the person making the request meant colonels and generals could have instant answers while nobody else noticed any difference.

7.5 Feature factories

You don't want objectives to specify a single feature, and you certainly don't want your list of objectives to read like a list of features you must build during the next period. And you really don't want a list of objective that just says 'Do A, B, C... Z'.

If you are regularly expected to just deliver one pre-specified feature after another, perhaps that is the way the world is for you, but maybe it also means OKRs aren't for you. While I wouldn't want to work in such a place, I know they exist and that some people think they are a good idea.

In such 'feature factories' the people doing the work have very little autonomy over what they do. Implicit to the OKR model – and explicit in agile – is that the people doing the work have a say in the work to be done. The workers get a say in objectives, and have latitude in how they meet those objectives and key results.

OKRs are not a good match for a feature factory. If you are running a feature factory, don't bother with OKRs and don't claim to be agile. Just hand out the work and tell people to stop complaining. I wouldn't recommend this approach: I think software teams work better when they are engaged, but it is your choice.

If you are running a feature factory then by all means set out a list of features to be done in priority order and tick them off as they are completed. Dressing the process up as OKRs may win some brownie points, but it will also take more of your time. Be honest: you want features, so measure features in, features out. Don't waste your time dressing this up as OKRs just because OKRs are fashionable.

However, even in a more enlightened environment where people are engaged in the work and have a say in what is done, there are times when there is just 'stuff to be done'. So you might set an objective such as:

> Do eight high-value backlog items

Although that reads more like a key result for a objective, so maybe the objective is:

> Deliver high value/priority backlog items

Even that could be better:

> Deliver priority backlog items for key customer accounts into production

Such objectives may be difficult to test – does one backlog item count as success? – but it does allow the team latitude over what they actually do.

It may not be beautiful, but it is possible. However, if you find yourself setting such objectives on a regular basis then consider it a red flag: something is wrong. Either your process needs to change or your attitude to the team does.

7.6 One for the team

In setting objectives and key results a balance needs to be struck between productive work – customer-facing objectives that directly deliver value – and work that increases the productive capacity of the team. The aim of this work is to build in future capacity. Such work might be technical in nature (for example, refactor database connectivity) or team-focused (for example undertake some team training), or something completely different.

The business value here is not immediate but is potentially greater. Capacity is being directed away from immediate value towards increasing capacity in the longer term. While I hope your superiors recognize and respect this, I know that all too often managers and even developers choose 'jam today' over 'more jam tomorrow'.

I encourage teams to adopt a hard and fast rule: one objective per quarter nominated by the team that will increase future productive capacity.

Without a formal rule, teams should be encouraged to suggest such objectives. Sometimes they will be included and sometimes not. But teams should also strive to improve their productive capacity in all the work they do.

Robert C Martin has likened this the boy scouts' rule:

> 'Leave every campsite slightly tidier than you found it.'

Specifically with code this becomes:

> 'Leave every source code file slightly better than you found it.'

7.7 Testing trouble

The objective might be more than the sum of the key results, so it needs to be testable in its own right. You need to be able to determine whether the desired outcome is met or not.

Herein lies a problem: time.

There are some objectives that take time to demonstrate. For example:

> Increase customer website visits by 10% over the next month.

It is entirely possible to achieve all the key result and do everything you think you need to do in order to increase website visits, but until a month has passed it is hard to know. While one could reduce the timescale (a week rather than a month), that might not provide a representative sample.

Alternatively, an OKR could be provisionally marked as 'achieved' because some key results were achieved and people believed others will be in time, but final judgement could be reserved for a later date. That could work, but then what happens if, when the day of judgement comes, the objective is not met? One might reopen the OKR and do more work, which could put the next set of OKRs in jeopardy.

Or maybe the objective is just not met. The team tried, they did some good stuff, but the objective was not met. It might be that a new OKR will be needed in the next quarter to reach the goal. Such an OKR would need to fight for prioritization against all the new candidates.

Ultimately it might not matter: things have moved on. The gains the team did make were an achievement themselves, whether they met the goal or not. Meeting yesterday's goal might not be that important any more.

In fact these problem are even more difficult than they seem. History shows that it can be very difficult to really measure the impact of technology change. The 1970s and 1980s saw large investment in corporate IT systems, but this was not visible in productivity statistics – indeed productivity growth seemed to slow during this period. Economist Robert Solow posed what became known as the *productivity paradox*:

'You can see the computer age everywhere but in the productivity statistics'[2].

Eventually productivity did pick up and the IT investments did deliver. In part this was due to the fact that investments took years or decades to deliver, but in part it was because economists were measuring the wrong thing. As much as we like to think $10,000 of IT improvements directly creates more than $10,000 of benefit, the actual benefit might not be quite as expected.

Finally, in part the productivity paradox was caused by the fact that process changes and management thinking did not change as fast as the technology. As every business analyst knows, getting the full value of technology improvements often requires process changes as well.

These same issues are at play when measuring objectives and key results: delayed effects, missing expected and unexpected benefits, and changes beyond the technology. So while one should strive for testable and tested objectives, one also has to recognize their limitations.

7.8 Take time but not too much time

When writing objectives, indeed OKRs generally, there can be a temptation to seek perfection. Indeed, when you look back at OKRs from the past, you can always see possible improvements. By all means aim high with both target and expression of OKRs, but don't let the perfect be the enemy of the good.

---

[2]Robert Solow, *We'd better watch out*, New York Times Book Review, July 12, 1987

By all means spend time crafting your objective and key result; don't rush the process. But also accept that your OKR could always be phrased better. Don't procrastinate when setting OKRs, a good enough OKR today is more valuable than an almost perfect OKR next week.

7.9 Summary

- Objectives describe the outcome you want to bring about.
- Objectives should inspire and don't necessarily need numbers.
- Make benefits blindingly clear and keep any background analysis and research out of the way.
- Team members to nominate one OKR each cycle to improve future capability.

8. Key results

One of the great mistakes is to judge policies and programs by their intentions rather than their results.

Milton Friedman, economist, 1912–2006

Writing key results might well be the hardest part of setting OKRs. Deciding on key results forces you to think hard and mentally explore the future.

Part of the difficulty with *key results* is simply understanding what key results are and are not. Past experience furnishes us with several models that can be mistaken for key results.

Key results are not stories that build towards an epic called an 'objective'.

Key results are not steps in a project plan.

Key results are not the result of the functional decomposition of the objective, neither are they layers of abstraction or components.

The secret to key results is in the name: *key results*. Imagine a future world in which the objective has been achieved, then ask yourself: *What are the important consequences of achieving that objective? What will the world look like after achieving the objective? What is different?*

If the objective is a thing to be constructed, what does the objective itself look like? What are the attributes of that thing? And the world that contains that thing?

You may choose to emphasize the greater consequences of achieving the objective, or you may focus on the thing – the product – itself. Either way, don't bother including the smaller consequences. By all means talk about them, but concentrate on the *key results*, the important things. The things you can see 'from 30,000 feet'.

It is useful to think of key results as tests that are used to see if you have reached the objective. Is the product big enough? Fast enough? High enough? Does the service meet customer expectations? If so, which expectations specifically?

Key results should be quantifiable – they should contain numbers. Numbers bring an objectivity to key results: remember that 'objectives are subjective, key results are objective'.

Adding those numbers to key results makes setting them harder, but doing so drives conversations and thinking.

Stating key results as quantified targets has advantages, as discussed here, but also disadvantages. The dangers of obsessive targeting are discussed in later chapters.

8.1 Test first

Apply the *test first principle* embodied in much of agile turns key results in *acceptance criteria*. Taking this approach a step further, *specification by example* can applied by describing the objective with a concrete example. This is particularly useful when building something new: get one that works first, then generalize.

Think of the objective as an example of what you want – maybe a certain level of sales, maybe a product, a customer response or whatever. Now ask *What are the attributes of that example that are most important?* Then ask *How will you recognize those attributes?* Continue by asking questions such as *How will they manifest themselves? How will you measure them? How will you know that those attributes have been achieved?*

Again, don't bother with the small things. You are only concerned with the *key results*, the attributes you can see from 30,000 feet.

When you take this approach OKRs start to look a lot like test-first management: tell me what you want to achieve, tell me how you will test whether you have met that goal. Apply the tests before you do any work: if you pass, then you are done! More likely the tests fail, but now you know your starting point. Work to fix the tests, work towards the goal, keep working until the tests pass.

If time runs out before the tests pass, stop. Step away from the keyboard and revalidate your thinking. Ask if the objective and key result tests are still the right ones. Maybe you have learned something that invalidates your original thinking. Maybe too much time has passed and you are better putting your efforts elsewhere. Or maybe something else has changed – the customer has gone elsewhere – and it makes sense to change focus.

Maybe, just maybe, the goal and tests are still valid and more time is justified. You might have felt that more time was justified all along, in which case you have been proved right. Arguably the time spent revalidating was *waste*, but those few hours of *waste* are only waste in retrospect. Pushing on without revalidating may mean you waste weeks pursuing an out-of-date goal.

8.2 Testable key results

When key results are the tests against which the objective is measured, it is important they are themselves testable. Some things are pretty much impossible to test:

> Make the site easy to use

or

> The site is secure

A little thought can turn these platitudes into testable statements:

> New users can complete a purchase on the site within five minutes without cursing

To test this one needs to find a potential customer and observe them. This could be done in your office, in the street or using an online testing service.

Doing the same for 'the site is secure' requires a bit more effort. What does 'secure' mean? Does the site run on https? Can it withstand denial of service attacks? Or SQL injection? Or a myriad of other interpretations of 'secure'. Further discussions are needed. Thinking about how you will test security can help to unlock what is required and what should be done.

8.3 Binary or analog?

The first benefit of putting numbers into key results is that they become more objective. Whether a site is considered secure or not might depend on the knowledge of the person doing the considering. But saying that a site can withstand a denial of service attack for two hours is an objective fact.

Another benefit of quantifying key results is that we can turn them from a binary all or nothing statement into a 'how much' analog measurement. Instead of a key result being done or not done, *some amount of functionality is done*. Some progress is made, some benefit is created, even if it is not as much as hoped for. For example, the ability to withstand a DoS for one hour might not reach the two-hour goal, but is still better than before.

Teams can make cost-benefit tradeoffs during the work. A website that can withstand attack for 100 minutes may miss its target by 20 minutes, but the team might judge it better to make progress elsewhere in the remaining OKR cycle.

Suppose a team can do 20% of the work to achieve 80% of the benefit, then why not? The work to achieve the last 20% might require far more effort. A 'near miss' on two key results might be more valuable than one hit and one complete miss. When a key result is a binary statement – all or nothing – such an option does not exist.

Consider a team coming toward the end of a quarter. If a key result is a large piece of work the team may not feel confident in starting it. Suppose they have two weeks left but feel they really need six weeks, what should they do?

If the key result is binary the team will get no credit for starting but not finishing. However if it is analog, then two weeks' work will make some difference; things will be better and the team can claim some credit.

Most of the key results mentioned so far are binary: they are either *done* or they are *not done*. If they are not done completely, then they are not done. In some cases that is all there is to it: something is done or not done.

Making results analog gives a team flexibility in how they address the target. Analog targets allow teams to aspire to a best-possible solution without mandating *nothing but the best*. If a highly aspirational target gets set in a binary form then, while the team may improve on the status quo, they may miss the target. When the OKRs are measured such failure makes the whole effort look wasted.

Analog goals allow teams to exercise more control; they have the option to stretch or to stay safe. This allows them to defer decisions on exactly what work to do and how to do it. It allows *just in time* decision-making before work commences. Teams can make these decisions within the same quarter rather than making plans in the previous one.

When a team starts to focus on an OKR and decide what to do, and again when work actually starts, they learn about the issue in hand. As they learn new options and complications appear, then binary key results box the team in: the team must do all the work whatever the complications. Analog key results allow for educated choices using all the information available at the right time. A working product with two out of three desired working features is far better than three features that are each 66% done and therefore all unusable.

8.4 Summary

- Key results can be thought of as the acceptance criteria for the objective. Thus they become test conditions and OKRs work as a type of test-first management.
- Key results need to be testable, but they are best when not all-or-nothing and can be partially met.
- Used like this, key results allow teams to know when they are done and make cost-benefit decisions.

9. Four types of key results

When results have dependencies, missing an early result jeopardizes later ones

Whenever one tries to suppress doubt, there is tyranny.

Simone Weil, philosopher, 1909–1943

Ideally key results are always quantified and analog: they are testable and form acceptance criteria to judge objective success – well – objectively. But the world is not ideal.

There is probably no one right way to write OKRs. There is no flowchart or checklist for creating key results. Broad principles and rules-of-thumb will have to do. Different goals will require different approaches.

Plus, being brutally honest, sometimes mistakes are made. Even when mistakes aren't made one can look back on past OKRs and say "I wish we hadn't done it that way", or "Now I look at it I see how it could be better". Because we are always learning, such things are inevitable.

It can be better to push on with a less-than-perfect key result than to spent excessive amounts of time perfecting one.

Still, I have come to identify four different types of key results, some recommended, some not recommended. It is also possible to see some crossover between them.

9.1 Type 1: Acceptance criteria

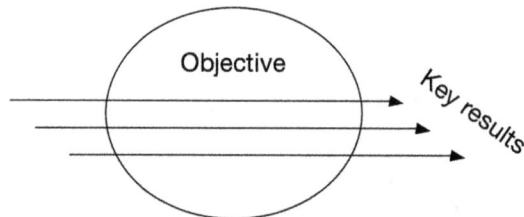

Key results describe attributes of the achieving the objective

Type 1 key results are attributes of the solution that need to be satisfied. Key results describe the criteria that must be met to satisfy the objectives. This view keeps the focus on the whole objective while highlighting important attributes of achieving that objective. Key results become *acceptance criteria* against which the solution is measured.

Imagine you are building an online store. The objective is a functioning online store offering a range of products that can be purchased and shipped directly to buyers. As acceptance criteria key results might specify: the capacity to list 1,000 items of stock with sub-second access times, a payment system accepting major credit and debit cards and an administration interface that requires no more than a few hours of training.

9.2 Type 2: Plan

Type 2 key results are most definitely not recommended. This model sees key results as a plan, as a series of steps to enact to build the objective. This style harks back to more traditional pre-agile working and describes both what should be done and the order in which it should be done.

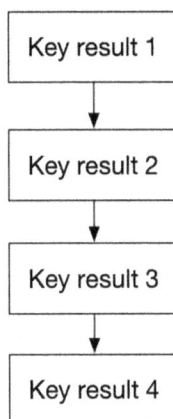

Key results as a series of steps

Building an online store with this approach might look very generic:

Key result #1: agree requirements for site

Key result #2: decide on software architecture

Key result #3: procure hardware

While this might be acceptable for a traditional team, in an agile setting it isn't. This approach will also increase risk: if the first step falls, then, like dominos, the others will be lost.

9.3 Type 3: Lego bricks

Type 3 key results are also not recommended. Here key results are seen as Lego bricks that, when stacked together in the right way, form the objective. The approach is essentially functional decomposition and the key results a form of functional requirement.

The Lego-brick approach to building a shop would have key results such as database containing catalog of items for sale, shopping basket, checkout, return and refund.

```
Objective
        ┌──────────────┬──────────────┐
        │ Key result 3 │ Key result 4 │
┌───────┴──────┬───────┴──────┬───────┘
│ Key result 1 │ Key result 2 │
└──────────────┴──────────────┘
```

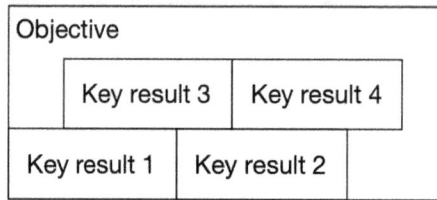

Key results stack to build the whole

This approach is problematic for several reasons. The domino approach means that if one brick fails, the whole objective is at risk. For example going live without a return system might work, but without a database all is lost.

By focusing on the functionality teams lose sight of the objective and the beneficial business outcome that is desired. This might seem attractive when teams are distant from their customers, but that is a problem that needs fixing, not accommodating.

Similarly, if teams are built around functionality (for example a database team, a Java team, a testing team and so on) it might be attractive to decompose the objective so that key results can be handed to individual teams. But in an agile world one should be reforming such teams, not accommodating them.

In addition, to achieve functional decomposition, someone needs to do the functional decomposition. This in turn implies a preplanning stage, which would reduce team autonomy, flexibility and motivation. In short this approach is not very agile.

Type 2 and Type 3 key results really aren't that different. Both describe a series of steps that when all executed correctly achieve the objective. Calling them out as different makes them easier to spot.

9.4 Type 4: Vertical slices

Type 4 is an improvement over Type 3 Lego bricks. This approach turns the bricks on their side and decouples them. It relies on the old agile technique of working in vertical slices: key results start to sound like user stories. Both aim to produce a valuable outcome, both represent tests and both exist in an agile context.

Objective: Online shop

Key result 1	Key result 2	Key result 3	Key result 4

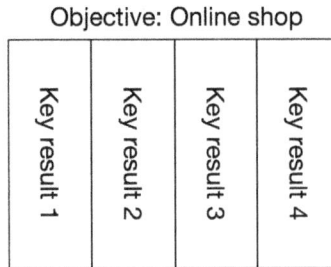

Key results are business beneficial vertical slices

Delivering value with each key result, just as with user stories, implies the target result is a vertical slice that delivers value in its own right. It helps too if the result is independent of other work; sometimes that isn't possible, but you should at least try and make it so.

Again this approach will be attractive to those who want to cascade work from one team to another, because key results can be split up. But this approach has limitations.

Consider the online shop example again. While one could imagine vertical slices such as payment system, customer account management, recommendation engine and others, how would any of these work without a catalog?

A catalog might be a vertical slice too, but without it the other slices are worthless. When results or stories don't stand alone, when they depend on another, then missing one imperils all subsequent stories. Like a domino run, if one falls, so does everything else.

Type 4 is almost recommended as long as it is used with caution. The aim is to realise the objective with a series of vertical slices that themselves bring benefit, but where the whole (the objective) is more than the sum of the parts.

9.5 Contrast

Types 2, 3 and 4 have the attraction that they describe separate pieces of work. This has attractions because work could be delegated to different people, even teams. Type 3 and 4 might even be run in parallel. The downside is that by decomposing the work, focus shifts from the objective to the work.

In contrast Type 1 key results keep focus on the objective. The difficult bit is to make each key result address different attributes of the objective, rather than having several key results that all basically state the same thing.

By decomposing the work early on, Types 2, 3 and 4 require more up-front planning. If this is to happen before the OKRs are confirmed more time is needed during the setting process for decomposition. Type 4 allows planing to be postponed until the OKR cycle has started – only then will a plan of work be formulated.

On first sight Type 4 key results may look harder to break down into action, especially actions that can be spread between different people. Consequently teams may spend more time in planning after the OKRs are agreed. It may also mean that teams need to work more closely.

The fact that Type 4 is harder to break down does not make break it down impossible. Certainly some key results may need to be addressed as a whole across all slices, therefore one design must work for results in all verticals. Others might be approached separately. For example, teams might still approach key results as different pieces of work; for example 'Make it work, then make it fast'.

9.6 Implications for cascading

For those who see OKRs being cascaded across an organization – something I don't recommend – then Types 2, 3 and 4 have an obvious appeal. A single objective can be set and individual key results peeled off and delegated to different teams. Each team then works in isolation and upgrades their given key result to objective status.

That Type 4 key results make this more difficult only makes the approach more attractive to my mind!

Having multiple disparate teams work on a single Type 4 OKR is not impossible. Assuming a mechanism can be found to have the teams agree on an objective, then it is a question of decoupling the key results from work items.

With the three other types, work breakdown is determined by the key results. With Type 4 work breakdown is an extra step that would occur once the OKR has been agreed. Only when the objective and success criteria are in place would attention turn to how it is to be delivered, and how the work can be spread across teams.

This has two advantages. First, in creating the OKR attention is focused on 'the business', or 'what the customer needs' and the benefit the objective will deliver. The technology and mechanics of delivery are secondary.

Second, as work proceeds attention is still focused on the objective. A single objective is shared by multiple teams and they are all working towards delivering benefit, rather than creating silos each of which focuses on their mini-objective.

9.7 Domino effect

With Type 1 key results you can miss one key result and still meet the others. With the three other types there is a risk of a domino effect: miss one and the others will fall.

Type 4 key results might avoid this problem if the vertical slices are sufficiently decoupled and customers recognize the benefits of those slices that are delivered, as long as the missing slices are not critical. Similarly, with Type 3 key results, if you are lucky the missing Lego bricks are at the top rather than the foundation. In this case something useful may be delivered, but with missing capabilities.

Don't rely on luck. Fight against dominos. Don't accept dependencies until you have tried hard to eliminate them. Maybe dependencies are unavoidable, but don't jump to that conclusion. Think long and hard.

If you do find that dominos are unavoidable, then double down on efforts to make key results analog. Binary all or nothing key results carry more risk than analog key results.

With 'binary dominos', when one falls the entire domino falls, creating a high risk that others will fall. When the domino is analog, risk is reduced. Partially achieving a key result may be enough for others to still succeed.

9.8 Summary

- Key results cut across the whole objective (unlike functional decomposition or user stories).
- Key results describe different attributes of the whole so that they may translate as different work efforts (pieces), or may cut across multiple pieces.
- Decouple key results so that failure of one does not endanger others.

Type 1	Acceptance criteria	Recommended
Type 2	Plan steps	Not recommended
Type 3	Lego bricks	Not recommended
Type 4	Vertical slices	Use with care

10. Objective worked example

All our talents increase in the using, and every faculty, both good and bad, strengthens by exercise.

Anne Bronte, novelist and poet, 1820–1849

Objective: open an online store by December 1 (Version 1)

Perhaps it would be good to make the benefit more obvious:

Objective: open an online store by December 1 so that Christmas sales will not incur fees from current service provider (Version 2)

Notice there is not a lot of detail about what an online store is. This is deliberate. Objectives that are short and sweet are better off than those crammed full of detail. Maybe someone has produced a big document describing everything required for this online store. That might be useful, but it doesn't need repeating in the objective.

Better still, trust the team. Ensure that the team members have the skills needed to do any required analysis or research, then trust them to meet the objective in the best way they can.

Most people have a clear idea of what an online store is: Amazon. This may or may not be right for you. If your store differs in some significant way, you might want to reflect that in the objective:

Objective: open an online prescription pharmaceuticals store by December 1 (Version 3)

This has the advantage of focusing minds and flags up that assumptions about the checkout process may well need rethinking.

However, the objective should not turn into a disguised requirements document:

> Objective: open an online prescription pharmaceuticals store by December 1 with direct links to doctors and pharmaceuticals wholesalers, payment and inventory management capability. (Version 4, not recommended)

While the store owner may want all the features of Amazon (catalog, shopping basket, payments, inventory management, dispatch notification, returns, wish lists...), listing them all creates several problems. Writing drives out conversations and collaboration and the team is constrained in what it can do: rather than focusing on an objective, the team now has a shopping list of features.

Neither objectives nor key results are meant to be exhaustive specifications. As with user stories, you want a flavour of the target, but to defer details until later. User stories are often said to be 'a placeholder for a conversation': a key result may need more than a conversation. Ideally that conversation is deferred until just before the work is done – *just-in-time.*

10.1 The date

Following the 'objectives are subjective, key results are objective' rule, including the date – December 1 – in the objective might be seen as overly objective; it is a number, after all. It may also be seen as redundant, as all OKRs exist within a timebox period. However there may be good reason for including the date.

For example, including the date might turn an otherwise unambitious objective – *open a store in the next 12* months – into a challenge: *open a store by Christmas!* The date may also serve to focus the team and customers on the compromises needed to meet the date.

Second, the business imperative to have a store open by December 1 may not align with the OKR cycle. December 1 may be before the end a cycle, or it might recognize that some of the work will fall into the next cycle.

While I generally interpret 'objectives are subjective, key results are objective' to imply that objectives should be inspiring and quantification-free, I'm not dogmatic on it. Sometimes numbers, including dates, can be useful.

Arguably 'delivery by December 1' could be considered a key result. In general I tend to prefer those constrains that need highlighting as key results (see below). As constraints go, dates tend to be in a class of their own, so I'm not dogmatic. If it reads best as part of the objective, then put it there.

10.2 Minimal?

While the Version 1 objectives don't say anything about how much functionality the store will have, they could be interpreted as 'open a minimally viable store'. Rather than leave this open to interpretation, the objective would benefit from being clear:

> Objective: open a minimal online prescription pharmaceuticals store by December 1 (Version 5)

Or perhaps the opposite:

> Objective: open a fully functional online prescription pharmaceuticals store by December 1 (Version 6)

Personally I'm not keen on the term 'minimally viable product' (MVP), because it is a moveable feast and means whatever the speaker wants it to mean. As an approach to product creation, however, the minimal approach has great advantages, and the same idea resurfaces again and again, whether a prototype, proof of concept, trial version, experiment or MVP.

10.3 Context and constraints

Notice that our objective doesn't say anything about the context in which the work is happening. It doesn't say anything about what already exists, how big the team is, the architecture, history or anything else.

As all objectives exist within a largely stable context, it seldom needs explaining in the objective. The objective stands on its own; it is short and sweet. By implication it says: "Starting where we are now, with the resources (existing people, product, systems and so on) and constraints that exist, this is what we aim to achieve".

One exception is where the team has other responsibilities, such as devops or 'business as usual'. This is discussed later; generally I encourage teams to expose such demands as OKR Zero.

One constraint is in the objective: a deadline, December 1. If however there were more dates, I would want to call them out as key results. For example:

Key result 1: Store is online and operational on December 1

Key result 2: Store is processing minimum ten orders per day by December 2

Key result 3: Store is handling 1,000 orders per day by December 10

Where context is not stable, or where constrains are changing, I would like to highlight that, most likely as key results:

Objective: Open an online store by December 1

Key result: Cloud processing fees increase by no more than 5%

Key result: Team onboards one new team member to increase capacity and absorb devops responsibility for live store

If it becomes necessary to record more constrains or explain the context – and I hope it isn't – then an appendix could be added. This would keep the objective and key results free from clutter.

10.4 Pharmacy

Let's mutate the objective slightly and make it more specific:

Objective: Open an online prescription pharmaceuticals store by December 1

One should note that in a real case there would be context. At the very least the context implies the jurisdiction: while the basic principle that doctors write prescriptions and pharmacies fulfil them applies in the US, in the UK and elsewhere the details differ. In particular, payment mechanisms differ.

Starting with this objective there are many possible key results. Web-based or mobile phones? Android, iOS or both? Digital prescriptions only? Or paper too? How much validation is needed? And what of payments?

So it might be worth considering the user journey:

A patient visits their family doctor and receives a digital prescription as an email with a unique code. When the patient visits the online pharmacy they can use the unique code to order prescription drugs. The patient will make an appropriate copay, after which the drugs will then be delivered.

The OKR does not need to include this user journey, but if it helps in setting the OKR teams may use analysis techniques as they find appropriate, such as user journeys, user story mapping, impact mapping, use cases or any other appropriate technique they are familiar with.

> Key result: One-off digital prescriptions are processed within ten minutes of the customer arriving at the website and customer receives drugs within 12 hours.

This key result is doing a lot of work, perhaps too much. It excludes reoccurring (such as repeat or refill) and paper-based prescriptions, places a usability requirement on the interface and goes beyond the team building the system by introducing logistics goals.

Assuming our OKR is for a team building the online prescription system, it may be too much to list delivery inside 12 hours. However it may be appropriate to acknowledge that something needs to happen for delivery. Perhaps another key result could be:

> Key result: Prescriptions are fulfilled through the existing company stock control and logistics system.

This key result lacks any quantification – it is binary: it works or it doesn't. So it is worth a closer look. Maybe there are issues to be considered: does the existing system have loading limits? Is there capacity in the team supporting the system, or does it need to be done with no impact?

As it stands the key result is a binary all-or-nothing statement. It is also a domino: if it does not succeed then the objective cannot be met.

10.5 MVP

A *concierge MVP* (use humans to do the actual work) could work, but only for small transaction volumes. So the question becomes: how many orders does it need to process? Assuming this is an MVP:

> Key result: Up to six prescriptions per hour are fulfilled.

This could serve as a technology demonstrator and provide for some market testing; it would even leave the option open of interfacing to an existing system. Assuming the trial was a success, another OKR, at a later date, would need to increase capacity and rebuild the interface.

Such an approach could be taken to almost any aspect of the system, such as prescription validation and payments. The only thing left would be a technology interface. If the true objective is to test the market for such a service, that might be acceptable.

10.6 Full-size

What if our starting point was closer to the Version 2 objective:

> Objective: Open an online pharmacy by December 1 so that Christmas sales will not incur fees from the current service provider.

Now the key result might be closer to:

> Key result: Up to 1,000 prescriptions per hour are fulfilled through the existing company stock control and logistics system.

Now there is some quantification; a system that could process 500 prescriptions per hour could partially meet the request. Still, there is a big risk, because without enough interface to deliver one prescription the whole thing will fall.

Turning to payments in the system:

> Key result: The system accept Visa, Mastercard and AMEX payments.

Again this is very binary. It could be restated as:

> Key result: Payments can be made using at least three major payment mechanisms.

Replacing the named systems with 'three' gives the team more flexibility to achieve the goals. While they may argue over what constitutes a major payment mechanism, they are also able to decide to substitute one, say one that presents particular problems, with an alternative.

10.7 What is key?

Perhaps more important than any of these somewhat technical points is to think about how the online system is superior to the physical experience, rather than that simply automating it.

From a customer's point of view, why would they use an online system over a traditional bricks and mortar store? It is not because the store takes Visa – that is expected. Nor does the customer care about capacity: as long as their order is fulfilled they don't care if ten or 10,000 other customers are served.

So perhaps the key results should say something about this:

> Key results: 70% of customers return to the online pharmacy within the year.

Or perhaps the online system can offer value-added services:

> Key result: Patients will receive reminders to take their medications.

> Key result: Weekly reports will be issued detailing medicine efficacy using patient reported data.

10.8 Summary

Notice the conversation I've had with this OKR, with myself, with the text and with you the reader. The process of writing OKRs will drive conversations about the goals and what is behind those goals. I've given an example and then questioned it. Perhaps as you have been reading you have spotted other things you would question. Perhaps you would have made different choices to those I made.

Throughout the search has been for more meaningful goals. The discipline of quantifying where possible makes it hard to set objectives and key results, but in so doing enriches the thinking.

The objective and key results here are not perfect, and I expect you can see where I've broken my own rules. But more importantly, there has been a conversation. If this were not an example in a book I would expect the team involved to be having this conversation and collectively improving the OKR.

In many ways the conversation is more important than the OKR, because it is in the conversation that people explore goals and challenges and become enrolled as part of the team.

No OKR is perfect: every OKR ever written could be better in some way. They are the best in the time available. The final OKR serves to summarize the conversation and agreements that have come about. Next it serves to focus attention and remind the team of the discussion.

11. Measuring

Managers who don't know how to measure what they want settle for wanting what they can measure. For example, those who want a high quality of work life but don't know how to measure it often settle for wanting a high standard of living because they can measure it.

Russell L Ackoff, 1919–2009, management professor and organizational theorist

Last quarter's OKRs were projected on to the screen of the small room. Most of the team and two more senior managers gathered around the screen for the review.

Each objective and key result was rationally examined. Those which were clearly quantified were easy to tick or cross. Others required a judgement call preceded by discussion. These discussions usually ended with someone, usually one of the managers, saying "Shall we call it 80% done then?"

At the end the most senior manager summed it up: "Shall we call it 75% overall?". Nobody objected. For all the rationality, it came down to that: someone's judgement.

Quantifying a goal is hard. Even when measurements look easy, teams need to agree how to measure the goal. You may use the same measurements you first thought of, but discussing the measurements as a team will increase understanding of both the goal and the measurements. Rushing conversations about measurement is a missed opportunity, a lost opportunity to clarify what is really wanted.

Skipping quantification may seem like the path of least resistance when setting OKRs, but it stores up trouble. Without hard numbers and the discussions to decide those numbers, it is possible for individuals to hold different views on what the goal is and how the goal will be assessed. If the goal can't be measured, then at the end of the cycle success or failure is a subjective judgement.

11.1 Quantify

Objectives may be subjective, but the key results attached to each are quantified and objective. Thus the objective is quantified through the key results. So key results need to be quantified upfront. Ask questions such as:

- How will this be measured?
- What is the unit of measurement?
- What is the current value?
- What is the target?

It may be that you don't know these things when you set an OKR, or even when OKRs get approved and fixed for the quarter. Hopefully you do know beforehand, but if you don't then the first thing to do before you begin work on the OKRs is to work out how to measure them.

Measurement

'Anything can be measured. If a thing can be observed in any way at all, it lends itself to some type of measurement method. No matter how 'fuzzy' the measurement is, it's still a measurement if it tells you more than you knew before. And those very things most likely to be seen as immeasurable are, virtually always, solved by relatively simple measurement methods.'

Douglas W Hubbard, *How to Measure Anything*, 2010

If after a long hard think you still don't know how to measure something, read *How to Measure Anything* by Douglas W Hubbard[a]. Another good reference for software is Tom Gilb's *Competitive Engineering*[b]. In terms of ease of reading these two books are opposite ends of the spectrum: start with the Hubbard book.

---

[a]Douglas W Hubbard, *How to Measure Anything*, 2010, John Wiley and Sons
[b]Tom Gilb, *Competitive Engineering*, 2005, Elsevier Butterworth-Heinemann

11.2 Measuring the impossible

Faced with something that is hard to measure, it can help to ask *what are the desired attributes?*

For example, suppose you wish to measure software code quality. You might consider the following attributes[1]:

- Low defect count – that is, few reported bugs.

---

[1]Please keep your cool: I know some readers will spot the flaws in these attributes immediately. I know these measurements would raise my blood pressure, but please read on.

- Low cyclomatic complexity (McCabe) figure.
- A large number of automated unit tests.
- Engineers not complaining (too often) about legacy code or technical debt and requesting a complete rewrite.

Once you have the attributes you desire, consider how you might measure them. Remember, you don't need a super-accurate measurement – a rough one is better than none. To continue the example:

- Defects are normally logged in a database and a simple count made.
- Tools exist to calculate cyclomatic complexity for a given code base.
- Most unit test tools count the number of tests executed as standard.
- To measure engineers' complaints, buy a large jar and some ping-pong balls. Every time someone hears an engineer complaining they drop a ping-pong ball in the jar[2], then count the balls weekly.

For this example each of the attributes has problems – for example, reported defects correlate with the number of users. However, they are the kind of thing one might want to measure. Considering the attributes causes you to think more deeply: code quality is not necessarily an end in its own right: what is it about 'quality' that is desirable? Think beyond the label: what does the label, in this case 'quantity', mean in your context?

Some attributes may not have an obvious means of measurement. In these cases you need to think what your measuring tool will be – or as Tom Gilb would say, "What is your meter?". (Think gas or electric meter rather than metric meter.)

Humans have invented many measuring tools and units for the physical world: rulers to measure distance in meters or feet, scales to measure mass in kilograms or pounds, a variety of tools to measure the attributes of electricity: voltmeters, ammeters, ohmmeters.

The nature of software means that measuring tools often do not exist for the things you might want to measure. Software is written to solve novel problems using new technology, so the need for new measuring tools should not be a surprise. Measuring novel solutions frequently requires novel measuring tools.

---

[2]Yes I know this sounds funny, but I've used ping-pong balls as a rough and ready measurement of key results in the past. While it might not be the most accurate measurement approach, it is certainly one of the cheapest and most fun.

11.3 Removing the subjectivity

The aim in measuring OKRs is to remove subjectivity and make them objective. Removing subjectivity is a powerful tool for focusing the mind and making goals clearer. However, sometimes subjectivity itself can be useful.

The time for subjectivity is when setting OKRs – *think broad*. Have the discussions, get the points out, talk to stakeholders, ruminate, consider different viewpoints. Then make a decision, commit to it and make it hard and fast with numbers and measurements. Pursue that goal for three months – *execute narrow*.

Stop, review, assess. Most of all: learn.

Feed lessons learned back into subjective discussions about the next cycle, then repeat.

Does that sound familiar?

Plan, sprint, review, retrospect... plan, sprint...

Or as Shewhart would say: plan-do-check-act[3].

There is a time for planning and a time for doing. Most of the cycle is spent doing, but there is time set aside for thinking, planning and learning.

11.4 Unintended consequences

So far so good: decide on the desired outcome and codify it as a quantified target. If one target might cause damage elsewhere, then include a counterbalancing key result. Allow the team to decide the best way of meeting the goals, and let them follow through on their own plans.

Except that – as no-one has perfect foresight – there is always a chance of unintended consequences. Too narrow a focus on meeting the goal and hitting the numbers can mean teams create damage elsewhere. Sometimes teams may 'game the system' and find ways of meeting quantified targets that do not produce the desired outcome.

Consider the code quality example again:

- Teams could choose to overlook or simply cease reporting defects to reduce the bug count.

---

[3]Also known as the Shewhart Cycle or Deming wheel, https://en.wikipedia.org/wiki/PDCA

- Cyclomatic complexity is not the only type of complexity in code: inventive coding could reduce the count while increasing complexity, or engineers may simply remove complex functionality no matter how beneficial users find it. Complex problems can require complex code.
- Having a large number of unit tests does not guarantee that the tests are effective or contribute to quality.
- Engineers could stop dropping ping pong balls in the jar, or learn to keep their mouths shut when others are around.

The ends do not justify the means.

As much as one strives to remove subjectivity in measuring OKRs, subjectivity is necessary to ensure that the means of achieving the goals facilitates honest results, and that problems are not created elsewhere.

Later chapters elaborate on these tensions and pitfalls.

11.5 Don't boil it down

When reviewing OKRs for success at the end of the cycle, it may seem attractive to boil them down. As in the opening example, someone may say "One out of four key results on one objective, four out of four on the next and two out of three on third, so 7 out of 11 in total – 64%".

Don't do this: OKRs are already distilled, so boiling them down to just a single number is a step too far.

Objectives are not equal: objective #1 is probably more important than the others. Some key result are more important than the others, some are easy to achieve, some hard.

Boiling it all down to a single number loses too much information, and does not say anything about the level of ambition or benefit actually delivered. Summarizing it all as a single number will only encourage teams to aim for a higher number. The easiest way to score 100% is to set OKRs that can confidently be met.

If you want to summarize your quarter, look to the benefit actually delivered, the value created for customers and stakeholders, then summarize that.

11.6 Summary

- Time spent qualifying OKRs up front will pay back in delivering the goals and in reviewing the final results.
- Quantification is hard and you may need to learn some new techniques.
- The OKR-setting process squeezes subjectivity out, but subjectivity needs to be added back when delivering, or *the law of unintended consequences* will make things worse rather than better.

12. Key result tricks

The first order of business is to try. You must try until your brain hurts.

Elon Musk, entrepreneur

When writing key results the temptation is always to write the obvious: 'Replace the payment screen' or 'Add new protocol XYZ'. If you apply the thinking outlined in the last chapter you should already be able to see some improvements here.

As you become experienced in writing OKRs, you will find that there are a number of 'tricks' that can be used to make key results more achievable while also giving the team more autonomy. As a result teams should find that they can aspire to greater goals because it is safe to fail.

This chapter outlines a few of the tricks I have found useful when crafting key results that are occasionally also useful for objectives.

12.1 Experiments

Of course you would like every key result to deliver benefit to the business, but sometimes you really don't know what will happen. You don't know if a solution can be crafted, or if the solution envisaged will produce the desired outcome. Traditionally teams would deal with such issues by undertaking pre-work, usually analysis and planning. But pre-work both detracts from the previous period and can be self-limiting.

Phrasing a key result as an experiment can be a useful way of attempting something with an uncertain outcome, or where the team is doubtful whether it can reach a goal. For example:

> Increase customer page views by 10%

Could become:

> Run three experiments to increase page views

Lest that sound too much like a plan of action rather than a goal to achieve:

> Learn about increasing page views by running three experiments and share findings

Or even several discrete experiments:

> Learn about SEO tool changes needed to increase page views with a series of experiments and summarize conclusions
>
> Compare page view statistics from ten experimental modifications to the home page and outline recommended practices
>
> Present measurements from 'other customers liked...' experiments added to pages

Notice the share findings' and 'summarize conclusions' appendages which, while vague, implies that the learning isn't kept in one person's head.

None of these experiments have measurable outcomes as success criteria. The measurements that are taken are information generated by the experiment. Success is doing the experiment itself and absorbing the learning that comes from it. Success is not reaching a target, success – the goal is to learn.

You could include another key result to enhance experiments to achieve a goal:

> Deliver 10% more page views using the results of experiments

While this risks creating domino key results – the experiments may not find a workable solution – some dependencies are acceptable and may be unavoidable.

The experimental approach also works when the team needs to tackle new technologies. Suppose a team has a web page it wants to make more dynamic, but lacks experience with the necessary technologies. The team might write a key result as an experiment:

> Ascertain workload and difficulty of replacing current pages with dynamic JavaScript by undertaking experimental replacement of XYZ pages

(Observant readers might notice the 'spike story' hiding in that goal.)

Phrasing a key result as an experiment makes it safer for the team to take on risk. The result of an experiment is learning: the team has learned something, and learning has value. That there might be working or even useful software is just a byproduct of learning. Even if there is no useful product, learning ensures that the team is in a better position to attempt the work next time.

Experiments mean that something is done, not that something is completely finished or finally decided. They just mean that something is done, the outcome is reviewed and learning happens.

Experiments can be particularly useful when dealing with people and process changes:

> Experiment with a new workflow and visual board

> Experiment with rotating on-call responsibility between team members; each team member should be on call at least twice

Experiments don't necessarily change things for ever, and one might argue that 'Learn ABC' is an action rather than a goal. So don't abuse this approach and welcome the challenges, so that you might find a better way still.

Still, experiments create learning and options; both have value. Our 'stock' of knowledge is increased, alternative ideas are investigated and information gathered before any final decision or commitment is made.

Some experiments are open-ended, for example 'What happens if there are more images on web pages?' Others test a particular hypothesis, for example 'Adding images to web pages causes viewers to engage more', or 'Adding images to web pages increases load times and reduces viewers'.

12.2 Hypothesis-driven development

Experimentation can be formalized by stating a hypothesis to be tested up front. Hypothesis-driven development (HDD) is described by Barry O'Reilly:

> *Practicing hypothesis-driven development is thinking about the development of new ideas, products and services – even organizational change – as a series of experiments to determine whether an expected outcome will be achieved. The process is iterated upon until a desirable outcome is obtained or the idea is determined to be not viable[1].*

---

[1]Barry O'Reilly, *How to Implement Hypothesis-Driven Development*, https://barryoreilly.com/how-to-implement-hypothesis-driven-development/, retrieved September 2020

Hypothesis-based experiments may require little effort and use existing capabilities (for example, '$100 spent on Google Adwords will result in over $100 of additional sales'), or they may require significant effort to arrange ('Android native app will generate over $10,000 in additional revenue'). Naturally, the less effort required to test a hypothesis, the more attractive it is to run an experiment.

Both objectives and key results can be phrased as a hypothesis to be tested by experimentation. Running a particularly involved experiment may be an objective in its own right. When there are multiple ideas for how to reach an objective, several hypotheses could be stated as independent key results, each could be tested, and the most promising used to reach the objective.

O'Reilly suggests a template for these experiments:

> *We believe* <this capability>
>
> *Will result in* <this outcome>
>
> *We will have confidence to proceed when* <we see a measurable signal>

When completed that might be a bit too long to put in the OKR itself, so you might put a short description in the OKR and the complete template in an appendix.

Stating an objective or key result as a hypothesis changes the success criteria. The outcome is no longer doing or delivering something, the outcome is learning: proving or disproving a theory. As long as the experiment is done, the outcome is met. Failure would be a failure to do the experiment, or the experiment itself failing.

Of course you probably want your experiments to work and the hypothesis to be proved true. However, disproving a theory can sometimes be more valuable than proving one. When an experiment proves something you already believe, you feel good. When an experiment disproves something, you need to find a new explanation, to learn more, and quite possibly to run more experiments.

12.3 Time-boxed

Careful readers will have noticed that several of the experiments suggested here are time-limited. *Time-boxing* is an old agile technique that can be used when setting key results. Like experimentation, it can encourage teams to take on risk or step into the unknown.

> Experiment with a new workflow and visual board for four weeks.

The idea behind time-boxing is that there is far more work that could be done than there is time to do it. Doing some of the work would represent an improvement, more work might still be needed for a complete solution, but the work done nevertheless makes an improvement. The goal is analog rather than binary.

Therefore rather than try to do everything, one can specify an amount of time that can be spent on an activity knowing that some – although not all – the benefit will be realized. For example:

> Spend one person-week improving the user interface.

Similarly, if you feel you need to investigate something before you decide, then time-box it:

> Spend three person-days investigating options to improve the user experience.

This ring-fences time to do the work, but leaves open the actual work to be done: deciding what is to be done is itself part of the work. It might be that day one is spent drawing up a short list of work options, followed by a group review, then someone actually doing the work.

Time-boxing is particularly useful when facing technical work that has no immediate business benefit, but potentially increases capacity to deliver work in future. For example:

> Spend two weeks of one person's time refactoring the feed polling mechanisms.

As with experimentation, setting a key result as a time-box changes the nature of result measurement. No longer is the benefit being measured, rather it is the fact that the work is actually done that is measured. Naturally this implies that one has be fairly certain that some improvement will result from the work.

I would prefer not to allocate large swathes of time like this where the business benefit is uncertain (for example, 'Whole team spends ten weeks improving SQL stored procedures'). Time-boxing can nevertheless be useful for striking a balance between competing demands.

12.4 Survey

Sometimes you want to make changes to people. Perhaps you want to address a problem that Product Owners in your organization have, or you want customers to see your product in a new light. In such cases you might want to write a key result that is tested by a survey. For example:

'Improve Product Owner communication by convening a fortnightly show-and-tell.'

Your test could be just 'show-and-tell took place'. That would be a very binary test (yes it happened/no it didn't), but it would not actually tell you whether the communications had actually improved. A survey might help here.

'Improve Product Owner communication by convening a fortnightly show-and-tell. Survey POs after third event and aim to have 75% agreeing that communications are better.'

You might combine this with the experimental approach above:

'Experiment with regular Product Owner show-and-tell sessions to improve communications. Aim to have 75% of POs agreeing communications are better after six weeks.'

While one could argue that an instruction to run regular show-and-tells was itself too restrictive, there is a balance to be struck.

'Improve communications between Product Owners. Aim for 75% of POs to agree that communications are better after six weeks.'

This key result could be criticized for being too vague. While it still uses the survey technique, it leaves open the question of what to do. Sometimes this might be the right thing to do, but sometimes something more specific is needed.

12.5 Knowing when to stop

If OKRs are going to be anything more than just statements of things to do, they need to have a clear end state: you need to know when you are done. Knowing when you are done is important because a) it allows you to move on to the next thing, and b) it allows you to take stock of where you are.

Concrete goals are great – 'Rank top on Google for OKRs searches' – but such goals can be very open-ended, and some goals are hard to quantify: 'Make all employees happy'.

Once in a while it pays to step back and ask if you are pursuing the right goal, assess your chances of meeting the goal and consider the costs of doing so. Time-boxes, experiments and surveys provide break points at which you can notch up an achievement and consider your next move.

That said, once in a while you might want to write an open-ended OKR (for example 'Fix as many bugs as possible this quarter'). Just be aware when you are doing this and ask yourself if there are alternatives.

Since OKRs are set, reviewed and reset on a regular basis, every OKR exists inside a time-box. Even the most open-ended OKR will get reviewed at the end of the quarter.

12.6 Summary

- Make sure you know how your OKRs are to be measured, and if necessary build the measuring tools.
- Phrasing results as experiments allows teams to take on more risk and enhance learning.
- 'Just do it' work can be set up as a time-box.
- Combine techniques and experiment with new ones to find what works best for your team in your environment.
- Think imaginatively about how you measure and learn from your own experiences with OKRs.

13. OKR cycle

The motto I'm advocating is: Let chaos reign, then rein in chaos. Does that mean that you shouldn't plan? Not at all. You need to plan the way a fire department plans. It cannot anticipate fires, so it has to shape a flexible organization that is capable of responding to unpredictable events.

Andy Grove, CEO, Intel

The word 'planning' gets overused; it pays to look behind the meaning. So when someone, even me, writes 'Plan OKRs for the next cycle', they might mean 'Set OKRs for the cycle', or they might mean 'Decide what needs to be done in the next cycle to deliver the OKRs (which have been set')'. Both are planning, but they are different.

I'd like to draw a distinction between planning that sets the OKRs and planning work to deliver OKRs. Both are needed, but it serves to see 'OKR planning' as a two-step processes: first set the OKRs – focus entirely on the outcome(s) you want to achieve. If it helps, just imagine everything is possible. Having decided on the outcomes you want to bring about, you can now proceed to the second step and decide on the work to be done.

This chapter looks at how to plan the work to be done. Other chapters in this section describe setting OKRs. While OKR-setting and planning cuts across all chapters, Chapters 17, 21 and 25 discuss it specifically.

OKR planning is a two-step process

Setting OKRs requires broad thinking. System thinking and design thinking are useful when deciding what goals to set. Deciding what work is needed is part of the narrow execution process. Systems and design thinking take a back seat – blinkers might be more useful to limit distractions.

13.1 OKR cycle

The OKR cycle begins, like a sprint, with a planning meeting. Only this planning meeting is not to break work down and schedule it, it is to set the objectives and decide on the key results. Indeed this might take more than one meeting, and will typically occur a few days before the start of the OKR cycle.

As with sprints, OKR cycles follow OKR cycles and there probably isn't a gap between them. This means that after the first cycle there is work to do closing off one cycle – review work, assess progress on OKRs and hold a retrospective – as well as planning the next set of OKRs.

But there is a difference. It can be hard to plan the next sprint until the current one is fully closed off. Although one shouldn't roll work from one sprint to the next, it happens, and stakeholders can find it hard to decide on priorities until they see what has been done.

I encourage teams to wipe the slate clean and start with a blank piece of paper when planning the next set of OKRs. Just because a previous OKR was only 85% done does not mean that 15% of the work rolls over. The 85% that was done is still valuable and should be delivered. When planning a new set of OKRs, teams should be asking "What is valuable today?", rather than "Which thing which was valuable ten weeks ago and still needs to be done?"

Consequently it is easier to think about the next OKR cycle during the final days of the current one. The tail of one cycle will overlap with preparations for the next.

13.2 Cycle length

It is traditional to run OKR cycles on a quarterly basis: 12 or 13 weeks. Quarterly thinking is common in larger companies: sales targets, portfolio reviews, personnel reviews and more all happen four times a year. So why not OKR cycles?

To start with, it is exactly because quarterly cycles are already busy that you might consider another time period. If you want full team involvement and senior manager's time, you will have a lot of competition. Of course one might offset quarters to reduce this: January, April, July and October for sales quarters; February, May, August, November for OKRs. It is still a packed schedule.

There may also be a tendency for these cycles to interfere with each other. Will sales targets or performance reviews distort OKR-setting and delivery? Or simply get in the way?

One option is to use a different cycle length. OKRs could be set on ten-week cycles. This would allow for five cycles per year with a two week break over holiday periods. Or perhaps three 17-week cycles?

When first starting with OKRs it can make sense to do two short cycles to practice the process. For example, two six-week cycles before settling into a regular ten or 12 week cadence. This would accelerate initial learning. Such an approach might also allow a team to synchronize with other teams who are part way through a cycle.

13.3 OKR-setting is not work planning

So far I have been keen to describe objectives as 'outcomes that you wish to bring about', or simply 'desired outcomes'. Outcomes are not in themselves work to be done. There will be work to bring the outcome about, but that is yet to be determined.

For some, key results are the work to be done. When you see KRs as (Type 3) Lego bricks that can be assembled into an objective, then OKR-setting and work planning are pretty much the same thing. Viewing KRs as acceptance criteria gives a different perspective: key results are not tasks and do not form a to-do list.

Objectives and key results describe the target end state rather than the route to that state. It follows therefore that in planning and setting OKRs teams are not assessing the work to be done. The primary task in OKR-setting is to decide the destination. Inevitably some discussion of 'Is it achievable?' and 'How will we get there?' will occur, but this should not dominate the discussion.

Particularly for teams creating ambitious OKRs, a gut feel of 'challenging but achievable' should suffice. If discussion lingers too long on 'what needs to be done', teams self-limit and become distracted from desirable outcomes. In other words: teams agree on what they can do rather than what benefits stakeholders.

OKR-setting is not work breakdown. Work breakdown happens after OKRs are set. This follows the 'right to left' planning approach advocated Mike Burrows[1] and Bent Flyvbjerg[2]. OKR-setting is 'outside-in' rather than 'inside-out': work from what is required back to what needs to be done, rather than what is to be done to what might be needed.

Within each OKR cycle teams run their regular agile method as before. Scrum teams run sprints, XP teams run iterations and Kanban teams hold replenishment meetings. The big difference is that OKRs are central to each planning. OKRs are not something teams do in addition to their regular work – OKRs *are* the regular work.

13.4 What about work planning?

OKR-setting and work planning is a two-step process. The first step, which needs to occur before the cycle start, is to set the OKRs. The second step is to work out what needs to be done. For this there are multiple options.

The simplest option is to wait until the work is about to be done. So the first Scrum/XP planning meeting of the first sprint in the cycle looks at the first priority OKR and works out what needs to be done this sprint. Teams can perform work breakdown, generate stories and tasks or use whatever approach works for them.

The team then repeats this process every planning meeting. This approach would certainly fit with the 'just enough' or 'just-in-time' planning philosophy, but it is unlikely to satisfy

[1]*Right to Left: The digital leader's guide to Lean and Agile*, Mike Burrows, 2019
[2]*How big things get done*, Bent Flyvbjerg and Dan Gardner, 2023

everyone.

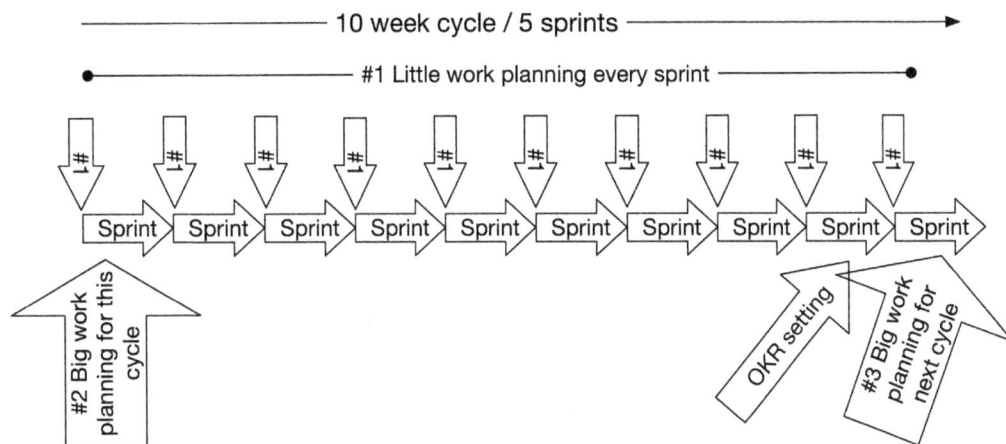

10 week cycle / 5 sprints

#1 Little work planning every sprint

#1 #1 #1 #1 #1 #1 #1 #1 #1 #1

Sprint Sprint Sprint Sprint Sprint Sprint Sprint Sprint Sprint Sprint

#2 Big work planning for this cycle

OKR setting

#3 Big work planning for next cycle

Three options for work planning

The second option is to use the first sprint planning to plan out all the work to be done. The team might confine themselves to one OKR at first and delay working on the second until the first is done. If the team needs to plan out work for multiple OKRs in parallel, they will probably need to address multiple OKRs.

When a team sees the need for a lot of work planning it may be better to hold a dedicated planning meeting rather than squeeze it all into sprint planning. The question which arises now is: should this occur before or after the start of the OKR cycle?

There is a logic to holding the work planning meeting before the OKR cycle starts. However, this steals time from the previous cycle, which might be difficult to spare. There is also a possibility that the OKRs might change before the cycle starts. Indeed, the earlier the work planning happens, the greater the chance that something will change.

The alternative is to put work planning right at the start of the new OKR cycle. Focus is increased because the previous cycle is finished, the time comes from the appropriate cycle and potential disruption is reduced. However, this 'just-in-time planning' will make some people nervous.

Personally, I tend towards the little-and-often approach, even if sprint planning meetings need extending. If more upfront planning is required I would avoid doing it in the previous cycle, to maximise focus in both cycles.

Estimation?

Once OKR-setting is separated from work planning it becomes clear that estimating work effort during OKR-setting is misplaced. To estimate the effort required, it is necessary to have some understanding of the work which will be done. So without even a high-level work breakdown, estimation is not possible.

Since OKR cycles are time-boxed, even asking "Wow long will it take?" is the wrong question. Rather, teams should be asking "What is possible within the time box?" and "How much can we do within the remaining time?".

For bigger work that potentially spans multiple cycles and even years a completely different approach is called for. Inside-out approaches – where the work to be done is determined, each item estimated and a total work effort divided by some denominator (work days, story points, the spin of a roulette wheel) is doomed to failure. Human estimation is problematic enough, but no work breakdown is ever comprehensive and those that try offer too many hostages to fortune.

Monte Carlo simulation offers some promise, but this needs historic data. Bent Flyvbjerg has pioneered an outside-in approach called 'reference class forecasting', but this also requires historic data.

13.5 Summary

- OKR cycles can be any length you like and the default 13-week cycle may not be the best.
- OKR-setting is not work planning. Work planning is a separate activity that follows setting.
- Work planning can happen a little and often at the start of each sprint, or it can be front-loaded with dedicated planning sessions. Preferably such planning should happen inside the cycle and not before.

14. Planning players

Brain-rich companies cannot be managed in the old asset-oriented style. Their managers have had to shift their priorities, from running companies to optimize capital to running companies to optimize people. In these companies, people are the carriers of knowledge and therefore the source of competitive advantage.

`Arie de Geus, The Living Company[1]

It should be obvious that the whole team needs to be involved when setting OKRs. These are the people who will have to do the hard work in delivering the OKRs, so it is only fair that they have a voice in their setting. Besides, basic fairness involving the wider team brings additional benefits.

Involving everyone in OKR-setting also demonstrates that all team members are valued: each team member can bring additional information and brainpower. Whether technical opportunities spotted by engineers or customer feedback from support desk personnel, all team members can contribute.

Allowing team members a voice in OKR-setting helps to enrol them in the process and the goals. Involved team members can be expected to be more motivated and committed to achieving goals when they have been involved with setting those goals.

Finally, involving more people in setting and planning allows those decisions to be put into action sooner. Some might say "There is work to be done, let people carry on working while other people do the planning. The planners can simply pass on the results." But such communication takes time and may lose information. Including the people who will execute the plans in the planning meetings means plans are enacted sooner.

In *The Living Company*, Arie de Geus describes how involving more people in decision-making actually leads to faster action. When everyone partakes in decision-making, they all share the decision and can move to action that much sooner.

However that does not mean that everyone on the team is equal. Some roles, specifically the Product Owner, have an extra responsibilities and play a key role in setting OKRs.

---

[1]Arie de Geus, The Living Company, 1999

Nor does the team-centric view preclude others. No team is an island; there are others to consider. If a team is to create value, it must deliver benefit to stakeholders outside the team. Few stakeholders will be involved with OKR-setting directly but many will be indirectly, to a greater or lesser degree.

While OKRs should be set *by the team and for the team* the benefits delivered by OKRs will mostly accrue to outsiders. Listening to what outsiders want, therefore, be they paying customers or senior managers, is essential.

Listening does not mean that outsiders get to impose OKRs on a team. Having someone outside the team impose OKRs will rob the team of autonomy, ownership and enthusiasm. But a team setting OKRs that bear no relation to the organization's aims and the priorities of others risks irrelevance.

Product Owner, Product Manager or what?

Throughout this book I use the term *Product Owner*. I do this not because I equate agile with Scrum. While the term Product Owner originates in Scrum, I do not believe Scrum is always the best way of working agile, or that OKRs are only applicable in Scrum environments. OKRs are applicable to any type of agile team, whether they are following Scrum, XP, Kanban, my own hybrid Xanpan or another approach.

When I refer to *Product Owner*, I mean the person who has the authority to make the final decision. In a product company this authority is often vested in a Product Manager. Inside a corporation a Business Analyst may be deputised to decide, or it might be a *Subject Matter Expert*.

While various types of managers may hold authority to make these decisions, those holding these roles (Product Manager, BA and SME) typically have specialist knowledge of what is required by customers and users. It is this specialist knowledge, which often comes from direct customer contact, which confers legitimacy to make 'what's next' decisions.

If there are no Product Owners in your workplace, mentally replace 'Product Owner' with the title of the person who makes these decisions in your environment.

14.1 Product Owner

Some organizations see the Product Owner as a kind of team leader. While the PO is certainly *a* leader in the team, they are not *the* leader. The PO does not so much tell the team what to do as lead thinking on what to do.

The Product Owner is a full team member and has a vital role in all planning discussions. The PO is the team member with the specialist skills and responsibility for gathering customer requests. It is the PO who undertakes product discovery, it is the PO who monitors competitors and it is the PO who talks most often to customers and other stakeholders.

Customer contact, skills and experience give the PO a special place and special authority on a team. POs have authority over deciding what the next thing to work on should be. When necessary, the PO has the authority to say *yes* or *no*. This extends to OKRs: POs will lead thinking, POs have the deciding vote and, if necessary, the PO can veto OKRs that provide no further customer value.

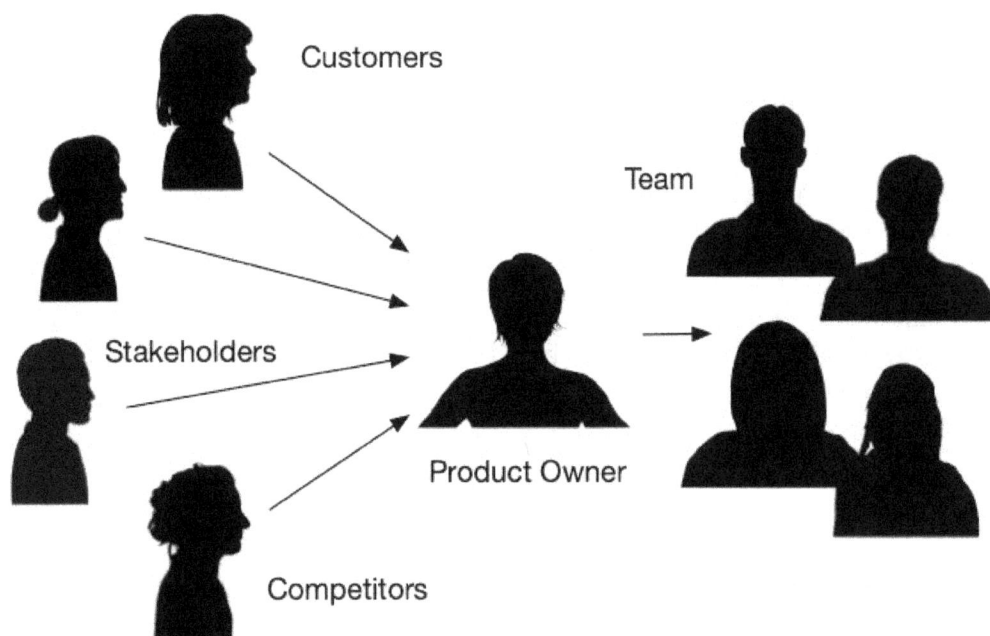

Product Owners have a special responsibility to listen to stakeholders outside the team

PO authority comes not from the fact that they occupy a particular position on an organization chart, or that others in the organization see them as *the leader*. Rather, a PO's authority comes from the fact that they are in contact with customers, they are the ones with the specialist skills and responsibility for understanding what customers and other stakeholder will find beneficial.

Product Owners are often assisted by other team members with specialist skills, such as business analysts, product managers, UDX experts and customer researchers. Such team members will also speak with authority, but it is the person with authority to make the final decisions who is the Product Owner.

Team members in any role will benefit from first hand customer interaction, whether it be customer visits, attending conferences or user groups or examining competing products. However, since their core skill set is not product discovery and analysis, these are occasional activities.

The OKR-setting process may seem never-ending to Product Owners. Like the rest of the team they will be involved with delivering the current OKRs, but they also have responsibility for thinking about the future. They should be thinking about what OKRs should be next, especially during the closing week(s) of a cycle. Indeed, suggesting OKRs is seldom a problem – the problem is more one of deciding what *not* to do.

14.2 Stakeholders

Outside the team there are many who will have an interest in what the team is doing and the consequences of the outcomes the team creates. Such people are stakeholders. Customers and users are stakeholders, parallel teams may be stakeholders, and so too are managers.

I can almost hear a certain type of hard-core agile developer ask: "We are a self-managing team, why do we have to involve stakeholders?" While some stakeholders might feel they have the authority to impose objectives and results on a team, this is not true of all stakeholders.

Acknowledging the right of stakeholders to have a view and make requests does not contradict the agile ideal of a self-managing team, nor does it deny the PO's role as the final decision-maker. Indeed, if a team is to maximize the benefit created and value delivered, it is essential to consider stakeholders' views.

The team does not exist in a vacuum – teams do not have a licence to do whatever they want. With sovereignty comes accountability. Delivering a successful product means listening to customers and other stakeholders, then trying to meet their needs within constraints.

Asking the views of stakeholders and listening to their opinion costs little. Involving them in the process is, again, simply fair play. They are more likely to respect and cooperate with a team that says "These are the OKRs we are planning to set, what do you think?".

In delivering OKRs teams inevitably hit impediments, and stakeholders can help to resolve issues and unblock work. Involving stakeholders increases leverage: stakeholders who have their stake recognized in OKRs are more likely to help.

The team is a mini-business unit – an amoeba[2]. Like any business the team ultimately answers to those providing funding – hopefully customers who buy products, but maybe other funders. Those who fund the team have a legitimate right to an opinion about what the team should be building. So to do other legitimate stakeholders, although those who control the money tend to get a bigger say.

Money not only funds the team, but is a valuable form of feedback. In the extreme, if the team does not listen to feedback, money also offers control.

The activity called 'planning' serves to integrate different views and demands for the work the team will do. Undertaking planning provides a forum to air opinions and agree shared priorities.

It is safe to assume that team members care about the product and what is delivered. Further, it is reasonable to assume that members care about the product's success. Since success derives from the product's ability to deliver benefit to customers and other stakeholders, it is logical to assume that team members want to achieve this.

Thus the interests of team members, customers and other stakeholders align. Contrary to some stereotypes, engineers' interests do conform with those of their customers.

With infinite time and resources everyone could be satisfied, but with limited resources there are inevitably tradeoffs. Priorities and opinions over how to allocate such resources will differ.

Creating and setting OKRs for the quarter forces discussions about what to do and what not to do.

14.3 Managers are stakeholders too

Where a manager – a development manager, line manager, project manager or whatever – is responsible for the team, then they are a team member. As a team member they need to be part of the OKR-setting process: they are as responsible for delivering the OKRs as anyone else. Being a manager does not give them the right to mandate OKRs, but neither is it reason to exclude them.

Other managers may not be team members, but are stakeholders in what the team does and delivers. This might not give them the right to tell a team what to do, but it does mean they have a right to have their requests listened to. Some of these stakeholders will have more authority and influence than others and might be able to force a decision.

[2] *Amoeba Management*, Kazuo Inamori, 1999

In addition there are likely to be what I call 'non-commissioned managers'. For example, Product Owners and Scrum Masters from other teams, who may not hold a position in the management hierarchy, but whose role confers more legitimacy and influence.

Problems occur when managers feel they have the right to impose their views and decisions on a team but teams don't share their view, or feel the decisions being forced on them are not the right ones. All concerned should work to avoid this scenario. Product owners should work to preempt the situation and such managers should work to explain themselves and find common ground.

Sometimes outright authority is needed; sometimes teams must be ordered to do something. However, when decisions are forced through regularly team moral and empowerment falls, motivation and productivity suffer. Decisions that are forced through with naked authority is a sign of failure elsewhere: someone had failed to explain themselves or someone has failed to listen.

Chapter 25 has more to say on the relationship between leaders and teams when setting OKRs.

14.4 Summary

- Product Owners and other specialists have the skills and responsibility to analyze what is needed; the technical team has the skills and responsibilities to create the solution.
- The interests of engineers, customers, financiers, managers and other stakeholders all lie in the same direction, even if opinions and priorities differ.
- Identify which stakeholders outside the team will have a voice in the OKR-setting process: other teams, managers, customers, governance and so on. Make sure your timeline provides time to include such stakeholders.
- Managers should not be imposing OKRs on the team, but neither should they be ignored.

15. Planning to plan

The process of planning is very valuable, for forcing you to think hard about what you are doing, but the actual plan that results from it is probably useless.

Marc Andreessen, software engineer and venture capitalist

In the same way that sprints have routines and ceremonies, so should OKRs. The OKR routine mimics the sprint routine – planning, regular refocus and retrospective. Both embody the plan-do-check-act (PDCA) model, often known as the Stewart or Deming cycle.

You don't want to plan your OKRs too far ahead – that would be a waste of time. But you do want to have time to plan them. Therefore plan to plan just in time. Planning and writing OKRs is the time to think broadly and ask big questions.

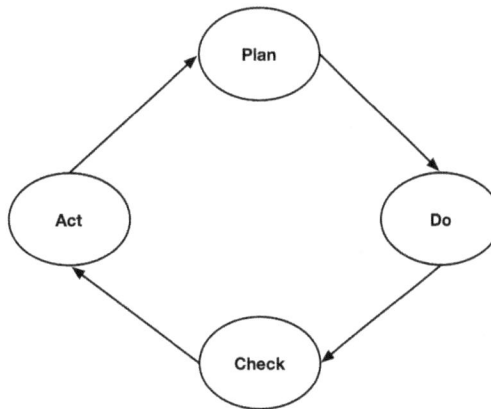

Plan-Do-Check-Act Stewart Deming cycle

PDCA	Sprint	OKR cycle
Plan	Sprint planning	OKR writing just before quarter start
Do	Sprint execution	OKR execution
Check	Review and retrospective	Review and retrospective
Act	Direct actions and input to next sprint	Direct actions and input to next cycle

The key is to sketch out a timeline for OKR-setting in advance, then plan backwards from the date the OKRs become live. Mark the events – drafting, review, stakeholder consultation and so on. Decide who should be giving input to the OKRs and who will be reviewing them. Get dates into peoples' calendars early.

OKRs should not be handed down from above – Chapter 25 discusses cascading OKRs. Nor should one person decide on OKRs and present them to the team: in an agile environment the whole team should share in the setting of OKRs. The team does not exist in a vacuum, however – it needs to listen to others.

Writing and setting OKRs is a whole-team exercise in which the Product Owner will take the lead. The PO knows better than anyone else what customers and other stakeholders want and need, and it is their job to bring customer requests and product strategy to the discussion. Other teams will make requests directly to the team or via the PO. Teams need to agree, both within the team and between teams, which of these are priorities and how they can address them.

Further, the team should expect to share and justify the OKRs it sets to its stakeholders. In particularly managers, as representatives of other parts of the organization, can reasonably ask for early sight of the OKRs, ask questions and suggest changes.

15.1 Schedule the events

For most of the quarter team members are narrowly focused on delivering OKRs, but when setting OKRs the opposite applies: thinking is broad and conversations deep.

Setting OKRs should not become a long-drawn-out process. It would be nice to think of a team wrapping the whole thing up in a day, but taking several days might be better. While spreading the process out over the latter weeks of the cycle works – see the illustration – I have come to prefer compressing the whole process into single week.

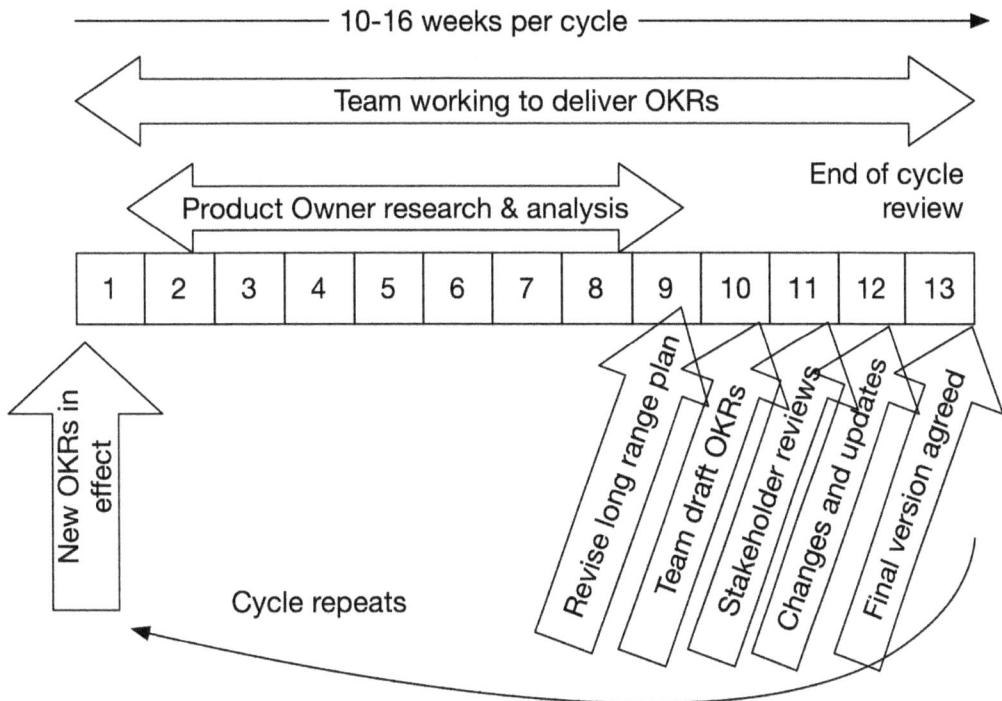

The OKR delivery and setting schedule may be spread over several weeks or compressed into one

Building in breaks, especially overnight breaks, allows for serendipity, individual reflection and sense-making. How often do things look different in the morning? How many insights come in the shower? Or walking the dog? People sometimes also find it easier to change their position when given time to think.

Consulting stakeholders will inevitably take time and slow the process down. Be prepared to iterate between team discussions and stakeholder consultations. You don't want such consultations to last weeks and weeks; having limited time and a deadline will keep things moving.

Involving the whole team in the discussion allows everyone to express concerns or highlight difficulties. Involving everyone removes the need to communicate decisions, so action can follow that much sooner. If team members do not have a voice in OKR-setting, they are unlikely to feel the kind of association and motivation they need to deliver them, let alone aspire to greater things.

In the initial discussions the Product Owner should set out and explain their priorities. Team members should also be able to make their own suggestions. Organizational strategy and objectives – the big goals – also need consideration, plus requests from other teams.

It is likely that there will be more ideas than can be accommodated. Techniques like dot voting can help whittle the list down to something achievable.

Where objectives are concerned, remember to start broadly, then take a second pass and look at the key results under each objective. This should be an iterative process, as key results for one objective may influence another, and some goals may overlap.

15.2 When to set

The bulk of the work drafting and agreeing OKRs is going to occur at the end of one cycle in preparation for the next. However, check that assumption: Christmas, Easter and summer vacations may mean that one cycle is slightly longer or shorter than another. Company reporting cycles, set events, conferences, shows and big-room planning may conspire to make one quarter 15 weeks long and another 11.

When an organization is new to working with OKRs it may not be clear when a cycle starts and ends. Pin down key dates in advance and agree them with others. This is particularly true if you are not following the common OKR cycle of resetting every quarter (13 weeks).

As with other aspects of agile, what is easy to say and makes logical sense turns out to require a lot of self discipline. Humans are good at working to deadlines, and routines provide a lot of structure and comfort, but establishing new habits is far harder and requires dedication.

OKR-setting events and reviews can get packed into the end of quarter. This may be distracting and intense, so there can be a temptation to start earlier and run a less intense process for longer. Avoid that temptation.

15.3 Start late

In setting new OKRs, teams need consciously to avoid distraction from delivery of the current OKRs. Deadlines focus the mind wonderfully, especially when they are close.

Starting earlier provides more time for talking, worrying and not focusing on the current quarter and its OKRs. It is far better to pack all OKR-setting activity into a short period towards the end of a cycle and allow most of the time to focus on the current OKRs.

Perhaps more importantly, things change. Starting the OKR-setting process earlier increases the chances that something will change between the first discussion and the last, invalidating decisions. Instead, remember the agile principle of the *last responsible moment*.

To leave setting OKRs beyond the last responsible moment – the first day of the next cycle – is, well, irresponsible. However, setting them too early invites prevarication and change, so allow just enough time and work intensively.

Setting OKRs late also helps focus during the cycle. Ideally, as the cycle draws to a close the workload will be lessening a little, as teams achieve some OKRs and discount others.

If the team intend to plan the next cycle's work before the start of that cycle then time needs to be allowed for this too. This will need to be squeezed in between deciding the OKRs and the start of the cycle. Obviously scheduling is easier when teams plan the work, including any design and breakdown inside the cycle.

15.4 During the cycle

While the team will look at OKRs throughout the cycle and ask "How are we doing? What should we do next to advance?", stakeholders outside the team should regard the team as a black box. OKRs go in, benefits, achieved objectives and new products comes out.

The team should certainly be highlighting achievements, publicizing key results ticked off and objectives met as they go, but the team doesn't want stakeholders asking "Are we there yet?" every few days. The team should not shy away from calling on stakeholders to help remove impediments and blockages, but to give regular – even weekly – status reports suggests stakeholders either do not trust the team or are more concerned about the appearance of progress than benefits delivered.

A live visual display of the status of each OKR in progress can go a long way towards answering stakeholders' requests for progress reports.

15.5 End-of-cycle review

At the end of each cycle the team and key stakeholders meet and review progress against their OKRs. While a team may strive to set clear, unambiguous and quantified OKRs, it is quite likely that some will turn out to be less than clear-cut and some measurements not work as expected. Someone therefore needs to make a judgement call on whether the team achieved an objective or key result.

Naturally reviews of OKR success should occur late in the cycle, to maximize progress and reduce loose ends. It can make sense to run such reviews back-to-back with previews and discussion of proposed OKRs for the next period.

The end-of-cycle review is a good time to hold a team retrospective. Rather than just focusing on a single sprint, the team can step back and consider whether current working practices are optimal and how they can be improved.

Since this retrospective will consider process against OKRs over multiple weeks, you probably want to create a timeline to help people recall the whole quarter. Allow this retrospective to run for several hours, rather than the 60 or 90 minutes most end-of-sprint retrospectives run for.

15.6 Mid-cycle review

Every sprint planning session is a mini-OKR review session. For teams who are not running sprints it makes sense to hold one or more team reviews during the cycle. With or without sprints, it can also be worth holding a mid-cycle review with stakeholders outside the team.

Such mid-cycle reviews can be an opportunity to update stakeholders and collect early feedback, especially if OKRs are unlike to be met. These can be useful to leverage stakeholders to help with impediments. But if mid-cycle reviews become finger-pointing micromanagement exercises, they negate the autonomy of the team and should be dropped.

Similarly, if teams are delivering regularly, communicating progress clearly and conducting demonstrations of new work, there might be a danger of over-reviewing. By all means conduct mid-cycle reviews, but only do so if they benefit both sides.

15.7 Summary

- Plan backwards: check key dates and sketch out your OKR-drafting and setting process in advance. Set key dates in the diary.
- Prefer a 'short and fat' intense OKR-setting process to a 'long and thin' process stretching over a large part of the quarter.
- During the cycle Product Owners should be busy supporting the team, visiting customers and thinking about the future, including potential objectives and key results.

III Working with OKRs

It's important not to overstate the benefits of ideas. Quite frankly, I know it's kind of a romantic notion that you're just going to have this brilliant idea and then everything is going to be great. But the fact is that coming up with an idea is the least important part of creating something great. It has to be the right idea and have good taste, but the execution and delivery are what's key.

Sergey Brin, co-founder of Google

16. Organizing to deliver OKRs

The absence of alternatives clears the mind marvellously.

Henry Kissinger

So you now have your OKRs sorted out and day one of the quarter has arrived – what do you do? How do you ensure that you give the OKRs your best shot?

Broadly speaking, there are two schools of thought on how to organize for OKRs.

The first school sees OKRs as additive: there is all this stuff that needs to be done, a backlog, business-as-usual, meetings and other daily shit. Work can come from many places: support desks and specific sales and personal objectives are common sources. OKRs are added as another factor in this mix without displacing any others.

Maybe OKRs are added as an extra list of things you should be doing, or maybe they are an attempt to bring order to the other stuff. Either way, backlogs still need to be burnt down, support calls answered and so on.

In this mode OKRs add more work to what is probably an already full system. Some sort of magical thinking makes people believe that OKRs are the missing ingredient that will bring harmony to everything else.

The second school of thought says that *OKRs are everything*: every decision and action is subservient to the OKRs. Don't even get out of bed in the morning if it doesn't contribute towards an OKR. Every story, every process, every decision flows from the OKRs.

As is often the case, these two descriptions represent opposite ends of a spectrum. The first school sees OKRs as a new way of injecting work, while the second see OKRs as the origin of all work and all organization. You and your organization are free to choose where on this spectrum you position yourself, but please recognize the spectrum and make a conscious decision about where you want to be on it. Set out clearly how OKR-driven work is prioritized against backlogs, BAU, support desk, sales and everything else.

Where are you?
Where does your work come from?

?   ?   ?   ?   ?

OKRs are one of   OKRs are
several inputs   everything

How are OKRs prioritized against other work?

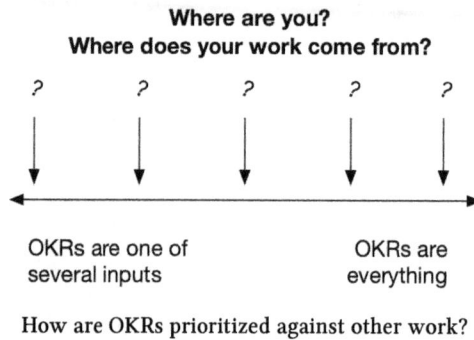

Having worked with OKRs I am in the second school of thought. To my mind, all decisions flow from the OKRs and build towards achieving their goals. Throw away your backlog, incorporate BAU into OKRs and don't do anything that isn't set out in the OKRs.

That might sound hard, but I see it as the power of OKRs. For three months they provide standing orders, a master strategy, agreement on priorities and a reference point for decisions.

One of the advantages of OKRs is that, because they are widely discussed, collectively agreed and shared, they serve to clarify priorities and connect strategy to execution. It is those priorities, the objectives and key results that drive all work: other work sources only dilute this power.

If you lean the other way, then hopefully much of this book is still useful. However you may want to skip some parts.

One word of caution: if your current methods of working are already difficult, if work is overflowing – too much is in progress – then adding OKRs to the mix is not going to help and may make things worse.

16.1 OKRs everywhere

Teams live or die by their ability to achieve OKRs. Team members shouldn't be scared of pulling discussion back to OKRs and asking "Will this contribute to the achieving the OKR?".

If you find that the answer to this question is frequently a 'No', followed by a direct order to do the work anyway, then seek to cover these eventualities in OKRs. If you still find those in authority unwilling to stick to OKRs they have agreed, then you may have a bigger problem.

Once you have agreed your OKRs, make sure they are posted in a prominent place. Don't just list them on a Confluence or Sharepoint page that people have to deliberately seek out in order to read – make them obvious. Write them big. Post them on walls. Put copies on the team board, issue printed versions to every team member – do whatever it takes to make sure they are instantly available.

16.2 Bigger team, fewer OKRs

People are frequently surprised when they ask "How many OKRs should a team have?" and I reply "Three, if you twist my arm then four, but really no more than you can count on the fingers of one hand." The shock only increases when I add: "Ideally, there will only be one."

Their surprise is often matched by my own when they say "We have 18 OKRs this quarter."

Sometimes they follow up by saying "We have a big team so we can take on more OKRs." However this logic is flawed.

Remember that much of the power of OKRs stems from their ability to create focus. Obviously having more OKRs means less focus. So too does having more team members: the larger the team, the more views there are on what the team should be doing. It is more difficult for team leaders, including coaches and scrum masters, to focus the team. Having more team members dilutes the responsibility of each individual and increases the possibility of distraction.

When a team is larger, rather than tackle more OKRs per cycle, the team should have fewer OKRs in order to increase focus. While a team of five might be able to work on three (or possibly four) OKRs per cycle, a team of 15 should accept only one or two.

When faced with a larger team with a diverse range of objectives to address I split the team into several smaller sub-teams. A team of 15 might be reconstructed as three teams of five, each of which has its own set of three OKRs per cycle. As a result focus increases, individuals have greater responsibility and outcomes improve.

16.3 Sprint planning with OKRs

As with so much else, work begins with the sprint planning meeting – let's start with iterative processes like Scrum, XP and Xanpan. If you are running an iteration-less process such as Kanban then adapt the ideas here to your cadence. The more dynamic prioritization process in Kanban will benefit more from OKRs than Scrum.

OKRs need to be central to each sprint planning meeting. Planning meetings need to include a full review of the current OKRs. Go down the list of OKRs and tick those that are done. The

Product Owner should then be able to direct the team to the highest priority OKR. It might make more sense to look at the objective as a whole, or to look at key results one-by-one; either way the Product Owner should give the team a clear statement of what is highest priority.

Avoid the temptation to 'do a little of everything'. Focus instead on one item and bring the collective brain power and energy of the team to bear on that one item. Focus exclusively on one item during the meeting before advancing to consider others – they are, after all, lower priorities. Involve everyone in the conversation.

If it becomes clear that the work to be done on an item during this sprint will not utilize the whole team, then advance to the next. During the meeting focus exclusively on this item until it becomes clear that work will not utilize the whole team. Don't waste time talking about OKRs that are not the focus of the coming sprint.

Aim to advance across a narrow front and achieve some key results before advancing to other objectives and key results.

Avoid pre-work if you can: a little bit of pre-work on objective #2 while focusing the sprint on objective #1 may look attractive, but time spent on #2 detracts from #1.

Agile is a team sport. As far as possible the whole team should be brought to bear on a very limited number of goals at one time – ideally just one.

Aim to work 'short-and-fat' rather than parallel 'long-and-thin' streams: that is – many team members working for a short period rather than having several work streams with one or two team members engaged per stream.

Avoid diluting focus by allowing experts to work on their chosen area. Peter might be the database expert and Rishi the Java expert, but starting two objectives in parallel because 'this one is for Peter and this is one for Rishi' dilutes focus and breaks the team ethos. Even if someone is less productive outside their specialist area, their work can still help deliver the whole objective sooner.

16.4 Traffic lights and status

It is useful to mark status against OKRs. This can speed up the review of OKRs, for example at the start of sprint planning, because the team does not need to consider items that are done and delivered.

Teams commonly attach traffic light status (red, green, amber) to objectives and individual results. Red signifies a problem, or that the objective/result will be missed. Green denotes that the team is on course and confident that the objective/result will be met. Amber is something in between: there is doubt or worry.

Personally I prefer a more fine-grained approach to status. The traffic light system does not clearly discriminate between what is green because it has been achieved and doesn't need any more consideration and what is green because it is on course and does require more conversation and work. At the very least a 'no colour' designation is needed to indicate work that has not started yet.

Although I have not had time to experiment here, I would suggest a designation like:

Colour	Status	Meaning
White (Clear)	Not started	
Yellow	Started, on course	Work in progress, confidence high
Green	Achieved	No more work needed
Red	Troubled	Work begun but problems encounter: time running out or technical issues?
Purple	Abandoned	Team has accepted the goal will not be achieved, no more work needed

16.5 Summary

- OKRs are it. Close your mind to everything else.
- The team exists to deliver OKRs: everything else is secondary.
- Find a simple mechanism to show the status of OKRs.
- Work short-and-fat through OKRs rather than salami-slicing them to work long-and-thin.

17. OKRs and the backlog

One never notices what has been done; one can only see what remains to be done.

Marie Curie

If you were paying attention while reading the previous chapter, you are probably thinking 'When everything is subservient to the OKRs, what happens to the backlog?'.

Basically there are two choices: write the OKRs so that they address backlog items and then, during the quarter, reverse the process. First the backlog drives the OKRs, then the OKRs draw the backlog.

Alternatively, *forget about the backlog.*

That might sound radical, but it makes for a simpler working process in which it is easier to focus on business benefit.

In crafting and agreeing OKRs each quarter, seek to deliver real value. Then, in each sprint planning meeting during the quarter, wipe the sheet clean and ask "How can we make progress on delivering our OKRs?".

Take Jeff Bezos' 'Day 1' approach: imagine this is the first time you have asked this question. Don't be constrained by previous ideas, previous work or sunk costs. Given the resources and time you have right now, what is the best thing you can do to move towards that goal?

Don't worry about whether your answer is in the backlog or not: OKRs are more important than the backlog. If you are lucky there might be some existing items in the backlog that you can pluck out and deliver, but don't count on it.

Plan the things you collectively think will move you towards achieving your goal, whether they are in the backlog or not. If you want to stay within the rules of Scrum, quickly insert the new items you agree on into the backlog.

Success is no longer burning down the backlog.

Success is delivering OKRs, or rather delivering business benefit summarized in an OKR.

The backlog is just a bunch of ideas, suggestions and things that might be done or, then again, might not.

17.1 OKRs, not backlogs

Agile teams, or at least Scrum teams, are accustomed to having a backlog – strictly speaking, two backlogs: the sprint backlog (work in flight at the moment in this sprint) and the product backlog (stuff that might get done in future.) On the face of it, OKRs represent competition for the backlog: *should the team work on backlog items or OKRs?*

Failure to resolve this question will result in certain failure. Those who measure team success by the amount of backlog done will see failure if the team delivers OKRs but not backlog. Equally, those who measure success against OKRs will see failure if the team delivers lots of backlog items and few OKRs.

The sprint backlog is less of a problem than the product backlog. The sprint backlog, by its nature, turns over rapidly. Work is put into the sprint backlog and, if all goes well, it is done within two weeks. The sprint backlog is normally loaded with a selection of items from the product backlog – which consequently 'burns down' (or at least, *should* burn down).

When working with OKRs it makes sense to choose sprint backlog items derived from the OKRs. Such work items might be key results themselves, or work items that will contribute to achieving the OKRs.

Either way, the sprint backlog is not the problem. Rather, the conflict is between existing product backlog items and doing items that build towards OKRs. Deliver an existing backlog item, or deliver something that moves you towards achieving a key result?

17.2 Backlog first

Broadly speaking there are two ways to resolve this conflict: *backlog first* and *OKRs first*.

Backlog first gives the backlog supremacy. In *backlog first* OKRs are guidelines for choosing work from the product backlog, while success is still measured by doing backlog items.

For example, if the key result you hope to achieve in the sprint is to improve usability, the team will comb through the product backlog looking for items that will improve usability, then put these items into the sprint backlog.

When crafting OKRs in the first place the team may examine the product backlog and devise objectives and key results that match the backlog. In effect the OKRs are reverse engineered from the backlog and OKRs becomes a vehicle for delivering the backlog.

Let's be clear: a backlog-first approach can work. But while it might increase focus, OKRs become a filter for selecting work from the backlog. Since the work is in the backlog, pre-work has been done; aspiration is limited to 'doing stuff in the backlog'.

By all means try this approach, but I've had more success with the OKRs-first approach.

The bottomless pit

For many teams, such as teams using electronic tracking tools, and especially teams using an electronic tool that begins with 'J', the backlog long ago became a bottomless pit, an endless list of work that might get done.

Backlogs inevitably grow; more often than not they grow faster than they are done. "Good idea, put it in the backlog" becomes equivalent to "Thank you for your input; forget it".

Growing backlogs are not a problem. A stream of work requests is a sign of success, as it demonstrates that customers get value from the product and want more. Unfortunately people still think that one day the whole backlog will be 'done'.

Work requests are not a problem. The belief that one day the backlog will be 'done' is.

17.3 OKRs first

An OKR-first approach measures success by achieving OKRs and delivering benefits rather than by delivering backlog items. The backlog is almost irrelevant: it serves as a holding pen for ideas, but it is not the only source of ideas. Teams are not bound by the backlog. If the team thinks of a way of moving toward achievement then the team can take it.

Certainly you will miss some items in the backlog, but if they don't build towards an OKR, are they worth doing? Not everything in a backlog must be done: items in a backlog are not promises, no commitment is made.

You might duplicate work: you think of work, write it out, schedule it, complete it and then discover there was already a backlog item that described the same thing. Such work duplication is wasted, but the time spent finding the item in the backlog and understanding it would also have been wasted. Items that are added to the backlog and never done are also waste. If something is a good idea it is probable that you will think of it again and again.

Maybe you'll miss important things. But if they are really important, how come they get missed? Maybe they aren't as important as you think?

A diligent Product Owner can conduct their own backlog searches during the sprint. They can weed out duplicates or items covered by other work, or pluck good ideas that help towards an OKR. This can all happen off line without wasting the team's time.

An experiment

Once upon a time I had a team working with OKRs. We had tried 'backlog first' one quarter, then decided to move to an OKR-first approach. The coach of a parallel team was wrestling with the same quandary. She decided to continue with 'backlog first'. At the end of the quarter we compared notes, and for the next quarter her team moved to an OKR-first approach.

17.4 Return of the sprint goal

Both backlog-first and OKR-first approaches revisit the idea of a *sprint goal*. This has always been part of Scrum, but is often lost in implementation. An OKR-first approach effectively makes an objective, or just a key result, the sprint goal. Work flows from that goal.

A backlog-first approach echoes the way many teams actually work: there is a lump of work to be done in the sprint. A sprint goal is invented to unify these disparate items; as such the goal is little more than 'do the sprint backlog'.

Personally I've usually found it difficult to make a sprint goal work, because the wider organization lacks clear goals. Outside the team, stakeholders 'just want things done'. OKRs present an opportunity to change this. Because OKRs are agreed with the business and represent business benefit, they offer the opportunity to connect the two sides over a shared goal.

17.5 Summary

- OKRs and backlogs conflict, because each represent demands on a team.
- A backlog-first approach can work, but is not necessarily the best way of working.
- An OKR-first approach means all work flows from the OKRs, irrespective of whether it already exists in the backlog or not.
- When taking an OKR-first approach, the product backlog is secondary.

I recommend an OKR-first approach: reset your backlog every quarter. Throw the product backlog away – you have nothing to lose but your burn-down charts. If you can't bring yourself to delete the backlog, then just ignore it. Lead with OKRs.

18. BAU – keeping the lights on

Every fighter's got a plan until they get hit.

Joe Louis, 1914–1981, boxer and world heavyweight champion 1937–1949

It turns out that business as usual (BAU) – answering help-desk calls, updating software, mending leaking roofs/fixing essential bugs, attending company meetings, line-management meetings, buying stationary and just 'keeping the lights on' – is problematic in an OKR-driven world.

In an OKR world people and teams exist to achieve goals: they don't exist to do all the boring day-to-day stuff. How can one have a goal such as:

Keep things working like last month.

Business as usual shouldn't exist. Much that is written about OKRs, and the way I have seen OKRs implemented, treats BAU as if ignoring it would make it go away.

Unfortunately business as usual *does* exist. Lightbulbs should last for ever, but they don't: they need replacing from time to time.

From an OKR perspective the problem with BAU is that it does not generate new business benefit; rather it supports ongoing business benefit. For a software team fixing bugs is BAU, but those fixes don't (usually) generate revenue or move the company forward. Customers expect the software to work and to continue working.

Once upon a time new product development teams could, with some legitimacy, fend off BAU because they existed to develop new products. The trend towards *devops* changes this: while *dev* may be mainly shiny new things, *ops* is mostly BAU.

For a consultancy group BAU is delivering customer projects, assignments and customer training. The business benefit was recognized when the deal was signed. Week after week they deliver stuff; it doesn't change the business.

So when senior managers look for objectives that will make the business better, BAU activities don't count. They don't generate new benefit, they merely continue the status quo.

This creates tension: business as usual lacks the glamour of objectives designed to improve the business and generate benefit. But the people who deliver those changes are also tasked with keeping the lights on; they only have 24 hours in a day, only eight of which are available to the organization.

There are several strategies for managing this tension.

Software always changes

In the software world there is a belief that once software is written, deployed and customers are using it, then the work is done. There is nothing else to do – everything is on automatic pilot.

This dream is a mirage. As much as one would like it to be so, and as much as one may work to get there, few teams ever experience this state.

The static nature of software means that while the world around it changes, the software cannot change without human help. Every change outside the software has the potential to require change inside the software.

For example: software utilizes third-party libraries. These libraries change and advance. If software is not updated further, change becomes more and more difficult.

Much modern software utilizes third-party services running elsewhere. A team might be able to defer a library upgrade for years, but if a service they interface with changes, failure to update can render the software useless.

Even software that doesn't use external services and libraries runs on an operating system and is build with software tools such as compilers and interpreters. The same issues apply here.

Nor is it only technical issues: successful software acquires more users, more users increase the variety of ways the software is used, thus more 'bugs' are encountered. Customers ask for changes beyond bugs. Keeping users happy, and keeping users as customers, demands that suppliers pay attention to their needs.

There are also malicious users: hackers, or more correctly 'crackers'. Even if your software does not have direct access to money, personal information, company or state secrets, a malicious user may find a way to hijack your system to attack another. So security needs to be maintained: using out-of-date libraries and operating systems opens doors for criminals.

If that is not enough, the world around software changes in ways that nobody expects. How many French and German programmers in the 1980s made provision for the Franc and Deutschmark to be replaced by the Euro? The 2020 Covid pandemic threw up multiple issues with software. US states were forced to bring Cobol programmers out of retirement to support social security systems.

The Euro, Y2K and Covid are big examples, but there are countless smaller issues which affect every system. Business as usual is about coping with these issues.

18.1 Option 1: suppress BAU

One answer would be to force BAU to go away. A team might deliberately choose to refuse BAU requests – not to change blown lightbulbs, not to respond to help desk calls, not to fix bugs on request and so on. In some cases this might be the right way to proceed: certainly it echoes some of the original writing on Scrum.

The logic here is quite simple: the priorities set in the OKRs are more important than the day-to-day stuff that comes along. While day-to-day problems may be painful for some, reaching the agreed objectives is more important.

Horrible as this might seem, suppressing BAU is a valid option. One might not like it, one might find it difficult to implement, but it is an option. Sometimes it might even be the right option.

This approach might work in the short term – I'm sure we can all remember times when we have pushed back. However, much of the work that is pushed back still needs to be done. Sometimes problems grow when they are deferred, such as an unhappy customer waiting for a reply. So while this might be a short-term solution, it should not be considered a complete fix.

Finally, any team pursing this option should make it clear to stakeholders, users and customers. Rather than just pushing back and pushing back, some explanation should be given.

18.2 Option 2: reduce or remove BAU

Google is the best-known user of OKRs. So, ask yourself:

'What would Google do if a team experienced BAU hindering their OKRs?'

Or to rephrase this thought experiment:

'How does Google deal with BAU?'

I don't know the answer, as I've never been inside Google, but as a thought experiment this is illuminating.

If like me your experience of Google is mainly as a search engine user or Android buyer, you will not have actually had much contact with Google. In fact Google's entire approach to questions, support and mass customer interaction seems to be: *make it go away*, perhaps by automation, by self-services, by community support or even by outsourcing the problem.

It is entirely possible to set an OKR to reduce BAU and ultimately even make BAU work go away entirely. So for example:

Objective: reduce the amount of time team members spend handling support requests on average from four hours a week to one hour a week.

Key result 1: Online frequently asked questions list (FAQ)

Key result 2: Website encourages users to find their own answer before a raising support issue

Key result 3: Community support portal allowing customers to answer one another's questions

18.3 Option 3: make BAU better

Some teams – for example help-desk teams – exist purely to do BAU. OKRs can be problematic for such teams, because they don't so much deliver new capabilities as keep the old ones working. To use a common metaphor, teams exist not to build the Forth Rail Bridge, but to paint it and continue painting it.

Such teams can still have objectives that add benefit to the company. These objectives probably relate to making the work better: more efficient (reduce time spent on issues), more timely (respond more quickly), better quality (increase customer satisfaction), more effective (reduce repeat calls), or, like option #2 above, concern reducing the work. Each of these desired outcomes has business benefits.

18.4 Option 4: objective zero – add BAU

When teams have nontrivial amounts of BAU and when failure to deliver it would cause problems – customers complaining about defects or customer installs not being performed – then I believe BAU must be recognized in the OKRs.

BAU absorbs team resources and gets in the way of achieving other objectives. Dropping BAU would be a retrograde step. Not acknowledging BAU – hiding it – obscures what the team is doing and the achievements they make – fixing ten bugs is an achievement, even if the bugs should never have existed.

However BAU is not like other objectives; it does not move the business forwards, but rather it stops the business from slipping back. BAU is more about revenue protection than revenue growth.

Therefore recognize BAU in the OKRs, but recognize it differently: it is *objective zero*. For example:

> Objective 0: keep existing system operation and customer issues within the historic range (say three to eight per month).

> Key result 1: help desk and developers respond to all priority 1 issues within 24 hours as per SLA.

> Key result 2: no critical security issues are open at the end of the quarter

> Key result 3: no software with less than three months until end-of-life is in production, and no necessary software updates are outstanding (including third-party libraries) at the end of the quarter

Such a *keeping the lights on* OKR would form a service level agreement between the team and the rest of the organization. The team would guarantee a certain level of service and then aim to achieve additional OKRs.

Having an *objective zero* keeps all the work in one place. It makes it clear to the organization what to expect and highlights the less attractive but time-consuming work the team is doing. Thus OKRs remain a single source of all work and 'change the company' objectives are put into perspective.

Teams undertaking BAU that is not reflected it OKRs might find objectives are missed because BAU is absorbing time. Acknowledging BAU within OKRs facilitates discussions about priorities and capacity. Teams and stakeholders can look at the OKRs and debate the balance.

18.5 Downside

What I dislike about suggesting objective zero is that it adds another objective to the team.

Having argued in this book for a limit of three or possibly four objectives per quarter, this potentially adds a fifth, or reduces the 'change the company' objectives by one.

As much as I dislike adding another, objective zero is my preferred approach to BAU, because it exposes the tension. Once exposed, this tension can be addressed openly. That said, I stick with the recommendation of a maximum of three OKRs, possibly four, but never five.

18.6 Summary

- 'Keeping the lights on'/business as usual complicates OKRs.
- BAU shouldn't exist, but does.
- In the long term teams benefit by reducing or removing BAU. Therefore write OKRs to make it better or reduce it.
- Don't let BAU lurk unnamed: agree a strategy to expose BAU.
- Expose BAU work with an *objective zero*.

19. Executing

Let me tell you the secret that has led me to my goal. My strength lies solely in my tenacity.

Louis Pasteur, biologist, microbiologist and chemist, 1822–1895

In an ideal world a team can work exclusively on their OKRs. There is no BAU (someone else keeps the lights on), team members have no history (nobody calls them up to say "I want to ask you about the thing you built last year") and no distractions – no company meetings, no support desk requests, no software updates, no performance reviews. In the most perfect world there would be but one objective for the quarter.

Back in the real world, teams struggle to keep focus on one OKR, let alone three or four. It is not uncommon to find a team has one objective to deliver product improvements (so-called *roadmap items*), another to create a customer-specific special and a third to improve system internals (reduce tech debt).

Executing against OKRs therefore means learning to have a laser-like focus on delivery.

19.1 Keeping focus

Maintaining focus is less about what you are doing and more about what you are not doing. Work requests that do not build towards your goals should be resisted.

When starting with OKRs, overcompensate: take ever opportunity to bring conversation back to OKRs and ask "Will this work help us achieve our OKRs?". This might make you unpopular, and you will want to throttle back before long, but don't let people lose sight of their goals.

Obviously the more objectives the team aims for, the more difficult it will be to hit any particular one. Therefore executing against OKRs starts when you are drafting them: limit the number of OKRs. Three OKRs should be the maximum, or four at most, but the last chapter outlined OKR-zero for BAU, which implies five.

Five is too many, so something has to give. Either face up to the problem when writing your OKRs, take the bold but difficult decision to cut the fifth OKR, or wait for reality to cut in and frustrate delivery of OKR five and perhaps one, two, three and four as well.

As Nancy Reagan used to advise children, "Just say no."

19.2 Prioritize

Early in the quarter, if not during their writing, you should prioritize your OKRs. *If you only deliver one OKR this quarter, which should it be?*

The Product Owner will have an outsized say in what gets done and what does not. Indeed, the PO may well be able to fend off day-to-day requests for additional work by themselves. When it comes to cutting an agreed objective or key result, the team should decide even if the PO suggests what to cut.

Stakeholders outside the team might have a say too. Although rather than wait for customers and managers to suggest changes, the team can make the first move. Asking stakeholders "How would you choose our priorities?" or "Which one would you drop?" allows the team to retain ownership of the OKRs.

The obvious approach to OKRs is depth-first: do one OKR to completion, then advance to the next, do that to completion, then advance and so on. Of course a breadth-first approach might be more applicable: achieve objective 1 key result 1, objective 2 key result 1 and so on.

There are countless permutations in between, so make sure the team has the discussion and everyone agrees the prioritization. Events will inevitably intervene and mean that some key results, no matter how important, are not delivered until later, but what you don't want is a random collection of key results delivered at the end of the quarter.

When a team has to deal with business as usual as well, whether acknowledged with an OKR or hidden away, then inevitably the best plans will be challenged. Similarly, when a team struggles with poor quality, problems can appear at any time. This all makes it more important to regularly pull focus back to the OKRs.

19.3 Visual display

Alistair Cockburn popularized the term *information radiator* when discussing agile teamwork. OKRs are a classic piece of information to put on your information radiator. The OKRs are the really important things the team is aiming to achieve, so make them easy for all to see.

- Don't post them on a Wikipage somewhere and leave them there.
- Do print them off and put them in every room.
- Don't talk about them in wishy-washy terms such as "You know that OKR about delivering the pizza function".
- Do walk people over to the OKRs when you are talking about them and point at the OKR in question.

The logical next step is to make the current status of each objective and key result a living visual thing. Teams running sprints have a visual status in their (Kanban) board, either physical or online. Similar mechanisms can be divided to show OKR status. A simple colour-coded wiki page is an obvious option, but I'm sure teams can find better solutions if they try.

19.4 Revisit often: sprint planning

Revisit OKRs on a regular basis and ask the question "Where are we at?". Reviewing them at every morning standup meeting might be going too far, but OKRs should be readily available so that you can quickly reference them if a question comes.

Reviewing OKRs at every sprint/iteration planning meeting – usually every two weeks – feels about right. The planning meeting is, after all, the time to review the team's progress and decide on the next steps.

If you follow my earlier advice to emphasize the OKRs rather than the backlog, then it becomes essential to review the OKRs at the start of planning to determine the work for the next sprint. Even if you can't bring yourself to abandon the backlog as I suggest, make sure you take stock of OKR progress over the last sprint and discuss what you will do to move forward in the coming sprint.

19.5 Time-slice

Earlier, when discussing how to draft key results, I suggested time-boxing. To recap, key results can be very open-ended: for example, to reduce technical liabilities in the system. A team could spend every day of a quarter doing just that and still have a mountain of problems to address. One approach is to say "Spend two weeks reducing technical liabilities". In so doing the team accept that technical liabilities, while reduced, will not be eliminated.

Even if you haven't done that explicitly when writing OKRs in the first place, you can still use this approach in executing OKRs. Not only are some OKRs open-ended, but there are multiple approaches to any given work item.

The time box may mean the ideal, perfect or best solution is not implemented, but any solution would be an improvement and move the team closer to meeting the OKR. Placing a time box, a constraint, around work can spur creativity.

For example, consider this OKR:

> Objective: shopping portal is online and customer can place orders.
>
> Key result 1: five item are available online for order (payments are accepted and dispatch notes notes issued).

If the team has all quarter to achieve this OKR, it may build an online store using third-party libraries. If the team has one sprint, it may subscribe to, say, a WordPress hosting service with sales plugins, then spend the remaining time customizing the site. Finally, if the team only has one day, it might set up a store Etsy, Shopify, eBay or Amazon Marketplace.

There is always more than one way to solve a problem. There is even a middle ground between the 'quick and dirty' and 'proper' approaches that often feature in discussion. The aim is not to build the best solution possible, but to build the best solution within the constraints, and the time available is one of those constraints.

19.6 Summary

- Keeping focus is key to delivering OKRs.
- Teams should use OKRs to say no to requests, distractions, diversions and other tumbleweeds that get in the way.
- Put OKRs where people can see them.
- Revisit OKRs on a regular basis and take stock of where the team has reached and what to do next.

20. Going off-piste

"I wish it need not have happened in my time", said Frodo.

"So do I", said Gandalf, *"and so do all who live to see such times. But that is not for them to decide. All we have to decide is what to do with the time that is given us."*

J R R Tolkien, *The Fellowship of the Ring*

If OKRs are to be effective it is necessary to measure all work against them: don't get out of bed in the morning if it won't move you closer to achievement.

OKRs can and should be a reason to say:

"I'm sorry Dave, I can't do that: my objective is to investigate the anomaly and the first key result is to put the ship into orbit."

In other words: OKRs are a shield that can be used to deflect those who would distract and obstruct your progress.

However, OKRs should not be a reason to act immorally, unethically or negligently, or to ignore events, changes and crises around you. Sometimes the right thing to do is to say:

"This is not in our OKRs but it needs attention. OKRs must take a back seat while we go off-piste. We will do it and work out how we pick up with the OKRs at the end."

Working only for OKRs is wrong, but so too is being too flexible and bending to every change and request. Teams need to find their own sweet spot somewhere between these extremes.

Writing this six months into the Covid-19 pandemic offers an obvious example. Teams that clung to OKRs without thought as workers were sent home, schools closed, internal travel ceased and countries locked down may well have been pursuing the wrong goals. Yet at the same time, some teams will have found their goals unchanged despite Covid once new working patterns emerged.

While many teams will have found themselves blown off course by the events of 2020, others will have found that having clear agreed goals provides stability in a turbulent environment.

Agonizing every day about whether the team is pursuing the right goals is a waste of time and energy. Equally, clinging to goals while fires burn and the world changes is wrong.

Sometimes a team needs to say:

> "Let's go off-piste, let's do what needs to be done. When things calm down we will regroup and assess where we are; which OKRs still make sense and what new priorities replace current goals."

It might be that when the crisis has abated the team can return its focus to OKRs, or at least a subset of them. Or perhaps the crisis has changed the world and OKRs need resetting. (Scrum aficionados may see a parallel here with the little-used *abnormal termination of sprint*.)

20.1 Unplanned but valuable

While OKRs can be a powerful means of keeping a team on track and reducing diversions and disturbances, some distractions are worth embracing, and not just because they are world-changing pandemics.

It should not be a question of 'planned work good, unplanned work bad', but 'what is valuable?'. If some unplanned work arises, the default position should be to refer to the OKRs and refuse it if it is not covered. But knee-jerk reactions need to be moderated: one should always listen to a request and consider whether it has value.

There is inevitably tension here, and both extremes are wrong: if OKRs are to mean anything, then they must mean that teams can turn down incoming work. But turning down all work because it does not build toward existing OKRs is equally wrong.

Ultimately the decision of whether to divert off-piste or to stay focused on OKRs will be a judgement call. There are no hard and fast rules on the right course of action, so all I can do is to make some suggestions:

- Is the thing being requested valuable in its own right? Is there reason to believe that it is more valuable than the current OKRs?

- Does the person making the request appreciate the consequences of doing this work and the potential knock-on effects?
- Is there time to consult other team members about the request? In particular, what does the Product Owner think?
- If you need to make a decision and there is no time or access to consult with other team members, ask yourself "What will others think?" and "If I do this, will I need to defend my decision, or will others agree?".

In the days when teams still used physical boards, I was known to write out the request on a card, take the card and requester to the team board and show them how their work request would impact others.

While any given request might be small, such as a bug fix a developer feels can be done in five minutes, one has to remember that even if it only takes five minutes, it represents a far bigger loss of time once mental context-switching time is added in. Then there is testing and release time to consider. Do not forget possible ripple effects and the risk of the fix going wrong.

Finally, remember that if one regularly agrees to 'small work', requesters will consider that to be the norm and will continue to ask for it. When given enough 'small work' that 'can just be squeezed in', then little of the strategic objectives will be achieved.

20.2 Prepare for the unexpected

One can never prepare completely for the unexpected, but teams can do some mental preparation, such as fostering a shared perspective on what should be accepted and what should be refused. While the Product Owner may be the one with ultimate authority, there are always circumstances in which individual team members will need to make a quick decision.

During OKR-setting teams might ask themselves to think of examples of work which, should it arise, will have priority over the OKRs. Similarly, the team could think of examples of work that would be pushed back and refused.

Such discussions can form part of team retrospectives. Teams might, in a non-threatening way, examine past decisions on unplanned work and consider whether the best decision was made. *Was the team right to refuse some requests? Were the accepted requests justified? What would have happened if a different decision had been taken?*

20.3 Track distractions

One way to approach the problem of unplanned but urgent work is to create a feedback loop, in true agile fashion. It might not save the day today, but it will help prepare for next time.

At the end of the quarter, when evaluating your OKRs and performance with stakeholders, ask them: would you rather the team had responded to fires and delivered fewer OKRs? Or should the team have focused even more and let others deal with fires?

In Xanpan[1] I describe how teams can track unplanned but urgent work in the same way that they visualize and track work planned in planning meetings. Basically they write out a new card – usually a yellow one – and put it on their board (physical or online) and treat it as any other piece of work.

If the work is really urgent it goes straight to 'work in progress', even if that displaces existing work. If it can wait a little while it goes into the 'to do' column until the next person becomes available. If it can wait a week or two it simply goes into the backlog for prioritization in the next planning meeting.

Importantly, by tracking the work teams can understand the nature of disruptions and quantify how much 'unplanned but urgent' work is asked of them – perhaps drawing a graph of requests per sprint. Over time the team can use this data to reason about the work: *Should they allow capacity in each sprint for unplanned work? Should they talk to specific people and ask them to submit requests before the start of the sprint?* Or maybe they need to remedy part of the system that generates unexpected work.

Teams using OKRs can do the same thing: count and track late-breaking requests that don't fit with the OKRs. This won't solve the problem immediately, but as the data grows the team will be able to reason about it and decide the best course of action.

For example, if the team regularly finds there are urgent BAU 'keeping the lights on' work request that fall outside the OKRs and cannot be ignored, then they may decide to adopt an objective zero to ensure such work is recognized.

---

[1] https://amzn.to/2MhFBm3

20.4 Summary

- There are times when clinging to OKRs in the face of change is wrong. It is better to go off-piste. This is a judgement call.
- If you go off-piste, regroup later and assess the impact on the OKRs.
- Cultivate shared thinking on prioritization outside OKRs, think about what might happen and learn from what does happen for next time.
- Track work that doesn't relate to OKRs, understand where the work originates and how it effects the team. Then decide what to do.

21. Beyond the quarter

We are not here to curse the darkness, but to light the candle that can guide us through that darkness to a safe and sane future.

John F Kennedy, 1917–1963, President of the United States

There are those who equate 'agile' with 'no planning'. Nothing could be further from the truth. There is plenty of planning in agile. Agile planning involves more people: the whole team is involved rather than a few specialists. Less planning happens up front, more planning happens *just in time*, so planning becomes *a little and often.*

Sprints plan for the next week or two; even when peeking into future, sprints only look weeks out. OKRs cycles consider longer periods, typically the coming quarter, but maybe ten or 16 weeks. Everything beyond the current cycle is subject to change. While you might sketch future cycles, nothing is promised or committed.

But beyond the next quarter? *Is it even worth planning?*

Planning is learning, planning allows us to visit the future, or at least one possible future. For some teams the future is so volatile that planning beyond the quarter yields little learning and is therefore of little value.

Yet for other teams longer-term planning can create valuable lessons. It therefore makes sense to plan for the future in order to learn about the future. However, teams should not invest a lot of time in such planning. As I describe in *Continuous Digital*[1], planning has rapidly diminishing returns.

However one plans, remember that the future is uncertain and plans will not unfold in the way one expects. Any plan is therefore simply a hypothesis of what might happen, while executing the plan – living the plan – is an experiment. Don't be scared to deviate from the plan if it creates more value than staying with it.

The further one plans into the future, the less the plan says about action and the greater the number of variables that can derail a plan. Short-term planning, planning your day, even planning a sprint, informs immediate action. Plans that look a year or more into the future inevitably lack actionable points.

---

[1] Allan Kelly, *Continuous Digital*, 2019

Initial rapid
learning period

Reduced learning from
additional planning

Marginal learning from planning time

0

Time

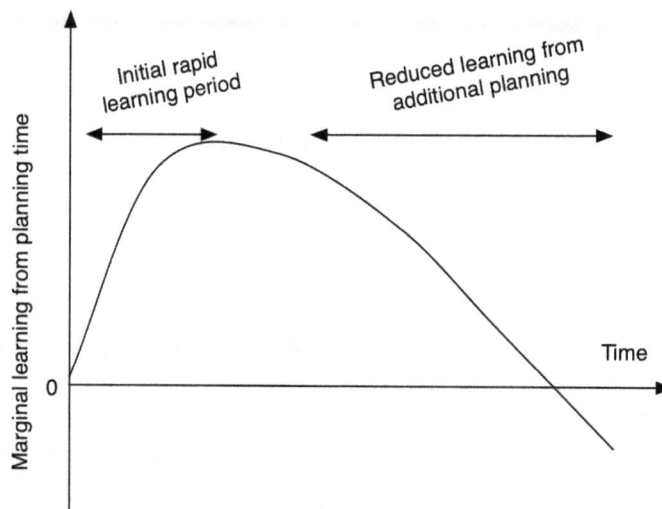

Planning has rapidly diminishing returns: a little is useful, but extra planning creates less learning

21.1 Three horizons

Agile teams benefit from planning on three time horizons. Very short term sprint planning, usually two weeks. A long-term horizon, typically a year or more into the future, and a middle horizon for which OKRs are well-suited.

Sprint planning is focused on delivery. Longer-term planning is concerned with deciding which outcomes are desirable. Or to put it another way, long-term planning chooses which battles to fight, while sprint plans focus on fighting the battles. In the middle planning needs to winnow the possible options and prioritize which outcomes and battles will be addressed next.

Scrum and other agile methods focus on short-term sprint planning. Product Owners nominate the work to do and teams plans how to deliver that work today and over the next two weeks. Sprint plans are action-oriented; they are action plans made by the team for the team to execute immediately.

Some teams stop there. They don't plan any further out, they live in the here-and-now. Sometimes that can be the right strategy, but most teams have some long-term ambitions, even if such ambitions are not actual plans.

Long-term planning looks beyond the sprint and current quarter. Such plans can run years into the future. Often called a *roadmap*, these plans are – or should be – collective efforts.

Such efforts should be led by the Product Owner and include other strategic stakeholders while retaining input from the delivery team.

Unfortunately, too often POs and teams are given plans created by others and then expected to execute them. Too often roadmaps are little more than a list of work-to-do with dates attached. Such roadmaps are worse than useless. Future deadlines can be useful, but dates based on 'estimates' are guaranteed to be wrong. Worst of all, it misses the learning opportunities that come from the shared creation of a roadmap.

While sprint planning is concerned with solution synthesis, long-term planning is largely an analysis activity focused on how the future may play out and what outcomes the organization will aim for[2]. Revisiting the roadmap and revalidating it weeks or months later is a rich learning experience.

OKRs play the role of 'planning glue' between long-term roadmaps and short-term sprint plans. Shared OKR-setting provides a mechanism for the team to decide which of the long term goals to tackle next and how to go about achieving those outcomes. At this horizon POs seek to enrol team members in their aims for the coming period.

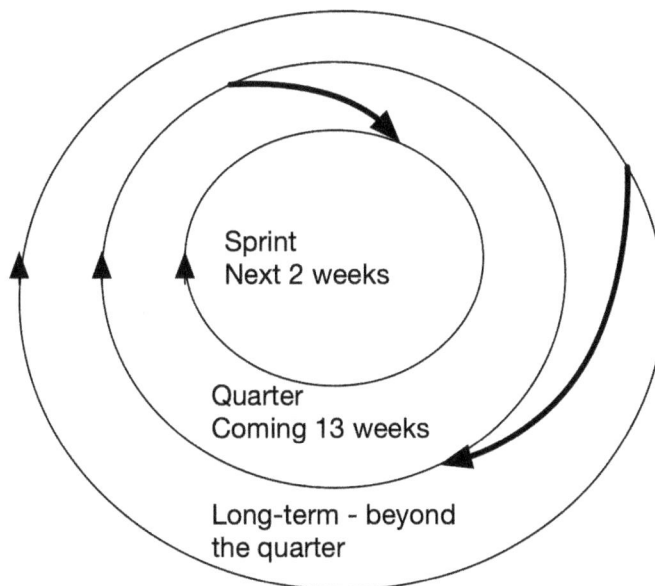

Sprint
Next 2 weeks

Quarter
Coming 13 weeks

Long-term - beyond
the quarter

Three planning horizons

So far this book has described how OKRs feed into sprint planning – that is, stepping down from a quarterly plan to weekly or fortnightly planning. In the general scheme of things this

[2]See *The Rise and Fall of Strategy Planning* (Mintzberg, 1994) for a full discussion of analysis and synthesis in planning.

is relatively easy: throw away the backlog and let OKRs drive every planning meeting as if it was the first and last sprint. OKRs become a backlog-generating machine for sprints. Agile teams with a high degree of autonomy will find this easier than those working to deliver someone else's agenda.

21.2 Rolling roadmap

Long-term planning is an ongoing rolling process – think of it as a moving conveyer belt. As one plan completes and drops off, another is made to take its place at the other end. Work trickles down from longer-term to more immediate plans. The long-term plan drives OKRs and OKRs drive sprint planning.

This rational machine-like planning process represents the ideal. Unfortunately, such an entirely rational view may be misleading – life is more complicated than that. Things happen, the context changes, plans must change too or become irrelevant.

Long-term plans are, indeed should be, in a constant state of flux. The long-term plan agreed in January probably looks out of date come April. Some of that is down to context: the world outside the plan changes; events like coronavirus change the world. Even in normal times companies shift money from one initiative to another, and customers buy or don't buy products in the quantities expected.

If the context were to remain fixed, then maybe one could sign off a long-term plan in January, then agree the January OKRs and those for April, July and October and relax knowing it was done for another year.

In reality the long-term plan is but one piece of analysis that inputs to the OKR-planning process each quarter. Finances are another big input, both financial plans and cash flows. Then there are things outside the organization's control: competitors, bad media exposure, national or international economics, government policy and more. Feedback on recent work and customers needs to be incorporated too.

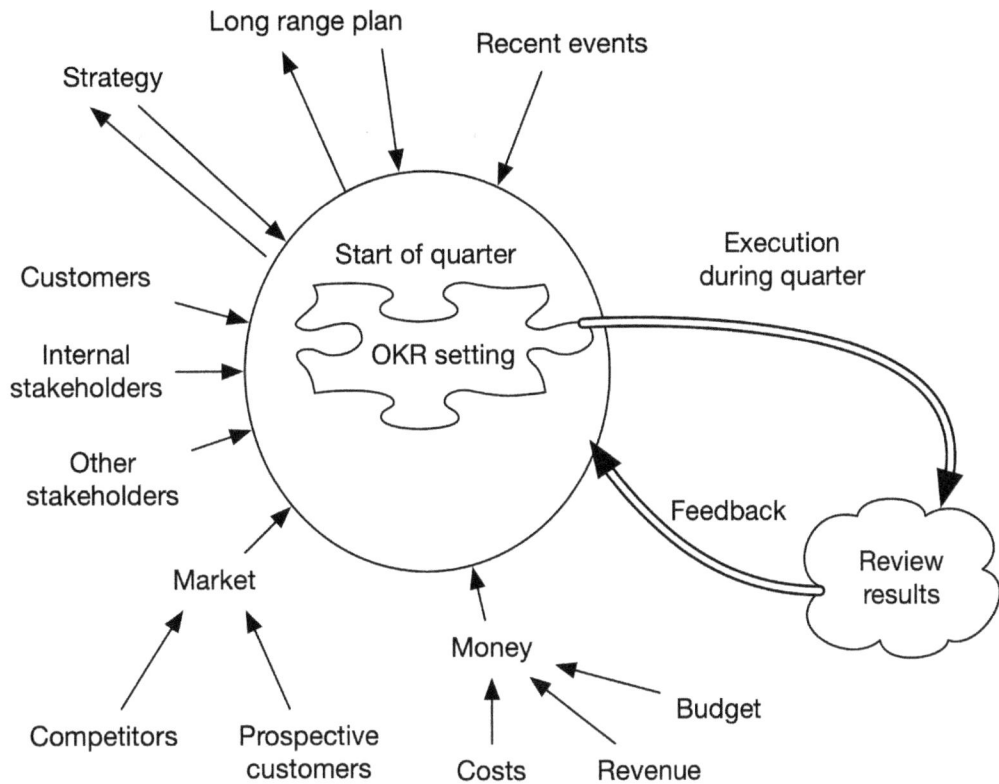

The long-term plan is one of many inputs to both OKR roadmap and quarter settings

The act of planning itself will change some of the inputs. Because planning is learning, undertaking planning will create insights that then inform and change both the long-term plan and strategy.

While the certainty projected by a plan may be comforting, in real life there are few prizes for staying on plan. Outcomes are the prizes. Long-term planning focuses on choosing the right outcomes, short-term planning on delivery of those outcomes.

The machine-like view of planning – long-range plans driving OKRs and OKR driving sprints – leaves no space for events, learning, feedback and change. Programming through planning defeats the ideals of agile and invites tragedy.

21.3 OKR roadmaps

One problem with discussing any planning further out then the next few months is the sheer variety of ways companies go about it. From the formal machine driven organization to the "think about next year when we get there" approach and everything in-between.

Where a company has an established long range planning approach then OKRs will be fed from that processes. Where it is absent, then the Product Wwner might lead stakeholders on an exploration creating an "OKR Roadmap" for future quarters. At this level the key results are too much detail, such a roadmap should stick to possible objectives in the coming periods. Any such plan would be a 'straw man', a possible scenario to facilitate discussion and not a detailed plan of actions to be taken.

An OKR roadmap should be actively promote options. In the same way a highway map shows the turning that can be take and alternative routes to a destination an OKR roadmap might show more possible objectives then would be undertaken. Doing so would allow the creators to visit several possible futures and learn from each.

21.4 Feedback

Most importantly, there needs to be space for feedback in an agile team: feedback from customers on the latest updates, feedback from engineers on how the raw materials are shaping up and feedback from the financiers who underwrite the work.

In fact, feedback from deliveries – that is, actual outputs – can change everything. Most obvious feedback from users and customers will affect sprint planning ("It's buggy!"), the next OKR set ("We love it, give us more!") and the long-term plan ("We would buy it if it was on Xbox").

But feedback can also change the way stakeholders feel about the product, cause the organization to make more resources available (or reduce them), provoke a response from external competitors and more. In short, feedback can go anywhere and effect everything.

21.5 Summary

- Think of planning in terms of three horizons:

    - Now: sprint planning looks a few weeks into the future.

    - Soon: OKRs look to the next few months.

    - Later: looking months and years into the future can create valuable learning. This is useful but things change, so don't expect plans not to change over time.

- OKRs act as 'planning glue' between long-term plans and short-term sprints.

Long-term planning facilitates learning through analysis and 'what if' thinking. The world will not conform to the long-term plan. Having completed a long-term plan one might as well throw it away: the real benefit is the learning in the minds of those who undertook the planning. Such plans would feed into OKR-setting and might be designed to show potential objectives to aim for.

IV Leadership

It should be noted in conclusion that management has a much greater impact on both companies and projects than almost any other measured phenomenon.

Capers Jones, *Applied Software Measurement*, 2008

The quality of the people on a project, and their organization and management, are much more important factors in the success than are the tools they use or the technical approaches they take.

Frederick P Brooks, *The Mythical Man Month*, Anniversary Edition, 1995

22. Strategy

"Would you tell me, please, which way I ought to go from here?".

"That depends a good deal on where you want to get to", said the Cat.

"I don't much care where...", said Alice.

"Then it doesn't matter which way you go", said the Cat.

"...so long as I get SOMEWHERE", Alice added in explanation.

"Oh, you're sure to do that".

Lewis Carroll, *Alice's Adventures in Wonderland*

When it comes to agile, many are like Alice. Agile is about the here and now. It is about being fast. It is about being responsive. As long as you are fast enough, as long as you listen to what customers are asking for now and then deliver it, and as long as you keep the system running and fix any defects the moment they are seen, then you'll definitely get somewhere.

Seeing agile as a fast and responsive system is a valid point of view. For some teams and companies it is exactly the right approach, but not always. Sometimes a different approach is better. Business people have a word for this: *strategy*.

But hang on, doesn't the agile manifesto say 'Responding to change over following a plan' – and isn't strategy a plan? Surely an agile team should always be like Alice and shun plans?

Not quite.

Responsiveness – especially when rapid and driven by customers – can be a very effective strategy, but it can also be a sign of cluelessness. Running around rapidly in circles might sometimes be the right thing to do, but it doesn't always signify progress.

OKRs highlight this question. A team could set OKRs every quarter to 'react to customer requests'. Setting such an objective would be a conscious act, and sharing such a goal with stakeholders would validate this decision. It is also possible that a team might find that, while stakeholders want a reactive team, they also want other things, things that are even higher priorities.

OKRs are both the product of strategy, because strategy informs which OKRs are set, and the mechanism through which strategy is delivered. OKRs can play the role of 'strategy debugger', because they make strategy visible. When OKRs don't support strategy it is a sign that something is wrong, perhaps because strategy has not been communicated, or perhaps because it is absent.

22.1 Big goals

The best agile teams certainly are reactive and should be, but that doesn't negate the advantages of having an overarching strategy. While I say 'strategy', you might substitute 'goal', 'purpose', 'mission', 'vision', 'BHAG' (big hairy audacious goal), 'MTP' (massively transformative purpose) or *strategic intent*. In other words, some *big goal* the team and perhaps the whole organization is aiming for.

However you formulate it, the important thing is to have an overarching idea. The idea might be a target, a goal to aim for, or you may have one or more principles that guide you in your work – a *true north*.

Strategy may be a place you aim to reach, or a way you intend to be. Feel free to choose. The important thing to realize is that a strategy is not a plan. Or rather, a strategy need not be a plan.

There are certainly plenty of companies for whom a strategy is a plan. For them strategic planning follows strategy formulation. *Strategy as a plan* is certainly one view: another sees strategy as a pattern of consistent behaviour over time[1].

This pattern may be a conscious decision: 'We will seek out large corporate customers who will pay top dollar for our product'. Or it might be emergent: one day you notice that the majority of your profit is coming from a few big customers who are paying top dollar.

Consequently strategy can be forward-looking or backward-looking. Strategy can help explain what has happened in the past. That might not sound immediately useful, but it is: recognizing (and naming) past behaviour allows one to either promote it in future or deliberately deviate from it.

---

[1] *The Rise and Fall of Strategic Planning* (1994) by Professor Henry Mintzberg is a tour de force that demolishes the idea that strategy can be determined in advance and then executed through strategic planning. The history of strategy and strategic planning has direct parallels with the agile-versus-waterfall debate.

Once you start to think of strategy like this, it becomes clear that a team that lives in reactive mode – "We don't need no friggin' strategy – we listen to customers and do what they want" – is in fact pursuing a strategy: a strategy of prioritizing customer feedback and responding rapidly.

This is a perfectly legitimate strategy, and may be the right one for many teams. But that does not mean that it is the only strategy, or that it is the right one for your team right now. By all means pursue a reactive strategy, but please make sure that following it is a conscious decision and not one you wander into.

Strategic intent

However you define strategy it has to start with a goal – even if that goal is simply to live in the moment and not make bets on long-term goals. Such a goal is free of 'how', it is not a plan, it may even lack a 'why' or a 'when'. The goal is the thing to aim for, sometimes called *strategic intent*.

As originally described, the idea of strategic intent fits well with OKRs. Rather than starting with the here and now and extrapolating resources and capabilities, strategic intent focuses on the goal, the outcome, the desired future[a].

Imagine you want to get fitter. That is your strategic intent – it is a goal. You might then devise a plan (for example 'join a gym'), set a deadline or allocate a budget. Or it might just seed a thinking process that informs future actions: eat more healthily, drive less, walk more.

On a visit to Starbucks a muffin can look very attractive. The value of one muffin is always more than the value of not eating one. No one muffin will add noticeable weight, neither will one stop you from losing weight and becoming fitter, but cumulatively it's a different story. But when there is *strategic intent* then the decision-making process is different.

Knowing the goal, the *strategic intent*, informs such decisions even without a plan. The muffin is rejected.

[a]*Strategic Intent*, Gary Hamel and C K Prahalad, Harvard Business Review, May–June 1989

22.2 Agile makes strategy more important

Having a strategy is actually more important for an agile team than it was in pre-agile working. Unfortunately, the ethos of agile too often means that teams pursue a reactive strategy by default. Teams, and in particular Product Owners, either don't consider strategy, or simply think 'agile' means doing what customers ask for as soon as possible.

OKRs form a link between the big and possibly nebulous strategy and the specific code-face work of agile teams. OKRs derive from strategy goals and feed into sprints. Think of them as a decomposition step if you like.

Agile gives teams the tools to be very reactive, but that very capability means that teams need to decide consciously how to use it. Being reactive is satisfying: acting on any given request makes you feel good. It provides feedback: you solved a problem and added value. But that doesn't mean it's always the right thing to do.

Think of it like a knife. When your knife is blunt, the effort required to cut something means you need to choose very deliberately which cuts to make. Since it takes time to make the cut, you have a little extra time to change your mind before the damage is irreparable.

Agile gives you a very sharp knife: you can cut anything with it, but that doesn't mean you should cut everything. You now need to think more carefully about what are the right cuts to make. The danger is that one gets carried away with making cuts and receiving positive feedback without realizing that the same time, energy and tools can generate even more benefit.

Strategy elements

It is common to talk about strategy as some god-like entity, all encompassing and indivisible. Perhaps the greatest strategies are like this, each individual piece forming a vital cog so that the whole is greater than sum of its parts.

That is not always the case. Often strategy is divisible and contains different elements – *strategy elements*. Some pieces are closer to the core than others, some can change without affecting the whole.

Surrounding the core strategy are multiple elements which, while they contribute to the whole, may vary. Things like financing models, the degree of outsourcing and technology platforms might be absolutely core to the strategy, or may be variable elements. Sometimes it is only in retrospect that one might see which was truly strategic and which was merely tactical.

22.3 Opportunity cost

Suppose you spend a day satisfying the requests of a single customer. You might feel great and you might deliver a lot of business value. But how else might that day have been spent?

Quite possibly doing something else with the time would result in even more business value. In doing X you do not do Y: the lost benefit of doing something else is what economists call *opportunity cost*.

Now this could – and in the past often has – become its own time sink. Fear of not doing the most valuable things can be debilitating. Faced with a dozen possible things to do, one spends time anguishing over which one is the most valuable to do now.

Unfortunately the clock is ticking: more time spent deciding on the best thing to do means less time to actually do anything. In the extreme more time gets spent analyzing and agonizing about the best thing to do than is spent actually doing the thing[2].

Again this is where strategy comes in. Rather than turning each and every 'what to do' decision into a long-drawn-out analysis, a strategy provides a filter. Instead of agonizing about 12 things, the list of things to do drops to four or five.

22.4 What not to do

A strategy doesn't just tell you what to do – more importantly, a strategy tells you what *not* to do.

The reactive strategy tells you not to make big plans, not to promise features to customers, not to make changes that impede future options and never to say 'No' to a customer request.

Conversely, a strategy that commits the team to targeting a few high-paying customers implies not responding to every customer request, not developing parts of the system used by low-end customers, limiting support and accepting that mass-market customers might criticize the product in public forums.

Suppose your strategy is to pursue growth in the US market. You may have many customers in Europe who all deserve to be listened to and helped. A reactive strategy would treat all customers similarly. But when pursuing a US-market strategy, European customers drain your resources. It may make sense to help those customer transition away from your products.

A stated strategy provides a guide for decisions and cohesion for the team and product.

---

[2]I keep a dice by my desk; when I spot myself falling into this trap I number the options and roll.

22.5 The backlog

Backlogs everywhere are full of more work than a team can do this millennium. Teams almost never burn down the backlog. Strategy allows a Product Owner to choose what to do or not to do.

What gets delivered is the result of a thousand small decisions. Without a strategy to guide the decision-making process, those decisions will lack cohesion; the final product – and code base – will lack cohesion. 'Biggest bang for the buck' works a few times but is short-sighted. Applied repeatedly, you may end up with a 'Homer car' – a bunch of cool features that collectively satisfy nobody but Homer Simpson.

Nor is it just backlog management that can benefit from a strategy. Teams themselves can benefit from having strategy and shared goals to focus thinking. Clear strategy and shared goals allows individuals to coordinate and align their efforts of these team members and share work more easily.

The software design benefits too. Strategy and goals inform design and refactoring decisions to create a more coherent design.

22.6 Don't forget the technology

Specifically, don't forget technical liabilities – what most people call *technical debt*. Having a strategy in place allows team members to reason about the technology solution and how its weaknesses will affect work. Having a strategy gives context to a conversation about how liabilities will be addressed, as well as the results if they are not addressed.

Technical excellence and consistently high quality are key strategy elements for agile teams. While some might see this as an excessively principled position, keeping technical quality high and minimizing liabilities is actually a pragmatic position that will lead to more efficient working and improved return on investment.

However, not everyone agrees that 'quality is free'. Each team must therefore navigate this issue for itself. Having an explicit shared strategy for the team, product and business must be a precursor for such navigation. Without a strategy to reference there is no common position to start from.

Technical liabilities

'Technical debt' is a misunderstood and overused metaphor. Debt has a good side: mortgages allow families to buy houses, credit cards make Christmas manageable, debt allows businesses to grow and governments to respond to pandemics.

Debt is often the preferred form of business financing, so to a business person 'technical debt' may well sound like a good thing. Engineers rarely perceive this interpretation, however.

Liabilities is a less ambiguous metaphor for everyone.

22.7 Shared mental model

Used like this, strategy becomes a heuristic that accelerates decision-making, particularly when agreeing OKRs. Stating such a heuristic allows sharing. No longer is the logic of decision-making locked inside one person's head: the whole team can share the same thinking.

While it is big decisions – strategy, OKRs, architecture, planning – that get the attention, every team member is constantly making many tiny decisions. What to call a function? When to make a function private or public? Is this a bug or a feature? Strategy and OKRs provide a guide when making decisions.

When people work together as a team decisions and actions need to be congruent. If the team is not making decisions that are in agreement, or members not acting in harmony with each other, performance suffers. At worst, in time the team may rip itself apart.

Strategic intent and strategy are foundations for high-performing teams. Teams that share an objective are more cohesive, work better together and have a better chance of achieving goals.

In an agile environment teams are more important than ever, so it is more important for them to share a common goal, common approach and common understanding. Quite possibly the benefit to the team from having a shared purpose is more significant than any of the other factors outlined here.

22.8 Summary

- The default agile strategy is for teams to be listening to customers and constantly reacting. This in itself is a strategy, but perhaps not the best one.
- Strategic intent, mission, vision, BHAG, MTP or just plain goal: it helps to have a common target.
- Strategy represents overarching principles and goals, makes a conscious decision as to how reactive to be, and acts as a filter to assist and accelerate decision-making.
- OKRs connect the overarching strategy with regular sprints. Rewriting them revisits the strategic intent and strategy.
- OKRs help to codify and communicate strategy and allow stakeholders to question that strategy.
- Strategy makes it easier to decide what not to do.

23. Leaders

All of the great leaders have had one characteristic in common: it was the willingness to confront unequivocally the major anxiety of their people in their time. This, and not much else, is the essence of leadership.'

J K Galbraith, economist, 1908–2006

Why do leaders have a role in OKR implementation? Because that's what leaders do: they lead. They can't lead if they don't believe; at a minimum they need to believe that it is worth experimenting with OKRs.

At first leaders need to enthuse people to try OKRs, then they need to support people through their first steps with them. If the OKR experiment is a success, the leaders' role changes – their focus shifts to sustaining OKR usage, deepening their use and achieving business goals through OKRs.

There is a school of thought that says that leadership is different to managing. There is a lot that one might discuss there, but not here. On a day-to-day level organizations expect managers to be leaders. Leadership is part of managing. A manager who cannot lead will find it difficult to fulfill their role successfully. Conversely natural leaders will find it easier to succeed at management.

For this discussion I'm going to treat the terms *leader* and *manager* as synonymous. If you find that unsettling, please read what I have written and ask yourself: for each point, is that work for a leader or for a manager?

Management is the medium through which organizational appointments can demonstrate leadership. There are other mediums in which individuals can demonstrate leadership, thus not all leaders are managers. For example, talented software engineers can become unofficial leaders within teams. Getting such unofficial leaders to embrace OKRs helps too, while unofficial leaders who are cynical about OKRs can be disruptive.

23.1 Culture, goals and strategy elements

Leaders have three big responsibilities in an agile and OKR-setting: culture, big goals and strategy elements. All of these overlap.

Leaders form and shape the *culture* of an organization. Leaders set the tone, norms and expectations, and model behaviours. Tone, norms, expectation and behaviours add up to culture.

Organizationally leaders – or perhaps even just one leader at the top of a pyramid – set the *big goals* the organization is chasing.

These big goals exist within a context. A big part of that context is the culture – the unspoken norms of how an organization works. But there are also spoken norms, things I would call *strategy elements*. For example, the core competences the company wants to grow, the degree of outsourcing used, when to innovate and when to milk a cash cow, office locations and funding mechanisms, to name only a few.

Culture sustains OKRs. Big goals need to be broken down into the smaller goals pursued by teams. Strategy elements enable or constrain how teams go about their work and the choices they make. Controlling the big three sets the context in which teams agree and deliver OKRs.

23.2 Day-to-day

Discussing and analyzing goals, culture and strategy elements can happen in isolation, but turning goals into action cannot. Taking action involves more people and more decisions. Much of a manager's work comes down to a myriad of day-to-day discussions, decisions and actions: it is in this that the culture gets lived, goals pursued and strategy elements implemented.

So it is with OKRs.

Having created the environment in which teams and OKRs exist, leaders need to support teams.

Leaders have a responsibility to provide the resources teams need to meet their goals, or to help them set goals within limited resources. Perhaps the most valuable resource leaders can give teams is their own time.

Leaders need to give time to teams: if a team needs to talk with a leader it is their duty to find that time. If the team makes a request – perhaps for more training, equipment, new team members or any other resource – the leader has a duty, not just to respond, but to do so promptly. If the answer isn't what the team wants to hear – and sometimes if it is – then the leader should also explain their response.

Responding to questions and requests is not just fair play: it shows respect for the team and acknowledges that it is central to delivery. In concrete terms teams can become blocked waiting for a leader's response: each slow response carries its own cost of delay.

When setting OKRs, a leader acts as both OKR expert and stakeholder representative. The team will most likely look to its leaders for advice on how to word OKRs and set targets. More importantly, leaders represent stakeholders and speak for the interests of others.

23.3 Leaders and culture

Creating and sustaining a culture is a bit like pushing on a length of string, and is equally unlikely to be effective. Simply telling people 'how it should be' will not work – although that is not to say that leaders shouldn't be explicit about what they want to create.

Leaders' primary tools for promoting a culture are themselves and what they do. It is not so much a leader's voice as their actions that will chart cultural norms. Living the attitudes and behaviours they want to promote allows them to provide a model for others.

If a leader cannot embody the culture they themselves wish to promote, what chance has anybody else? Saying one thing but doing another is a quick way to breed cynicism and undermine a culture. Employees will quickly spot discrepancies.

Leaders can promote culture by rewarding behaviours and actions that support the culture. Offering rewards upfront for exhibiting the right culture is probably not the best way to proceed. While such payments may well promote compliance, they will not *create* a culture. Once payments are withdrawn, people will fall back into their old ways.

According to some research, handing out unexpected rewards is a better motivator: reward people for what they considered *the right thing to do*, rather than pay them to do what you want. Certainly when team members expend unexpected effort, some acknowledgement is beneficial.

Rewards are good, but simple praise for individuals and teams is also powerful and far easier to give. Whether in public or in private, in group settings or one-on-one, saying "Thank you" can have an amazing effect. Simply acknowledging good work, telling people they have been noticed and appreciated, can have great benefit for promoting desired behaviours and attitudes.

Conversely, chastising people for poor behaviour or failure to match the desired culture is unlikely to change behaviour. More likely it will breed defensiveness, hinder openness and reduce ambition.

Over the longer term leaders can use the recruitment process to support the culture by hiring people with similar cultural leanings. Conversely, firing people can be traumatic and damaging to a culture, so removing poor fits should not be the first option. However, after every effort has been made, there may be people who would be happier outside the organization.

My big failure

One of the leaders in the Malaysian office took to rewarding his staff with meals out. In recognition of good work he would sometimes say to team members "Take your wife to dinner and expense the meal".

I was impressed. When two of my team members worked until midnight to meet a deadline, I was conflicted. Part of me said "No, we shouldn't be asking people to work that late", while part of me thought "Great, that's dedication!".

If I wanted to say "Don't do that again", I first needed to acknowledge and reward the team members. I asked my boss, Alf, "Can we give them a meal out?".

Alf said to ask Dietmar; Dietmar said to ask Jean; Jean said to ask Alf. So I asked HR. HR said it was against expenses policy. I thought about paying out of my own pocket, but that would have been me saying "Thank you" rather than the company.

23.4 Bottom-up more than top-down

A common view of OKRs is that, like MBOs before them, they are set at the top and cascaded down an organization. So the CEO sets the OKRs for the top team. Top-team members set the OKRs for their reports, who in turn set OKRs for middle management. The middle management...

Some advisors even go as far as to say "The key results at one level become the objectives of the level below". Once one views KRs as acceptance criteria rather than merely work items, such advice becomes folly.

This top-down approach is even advocated by some OKR advisers and writers. While this is one view of how OKRs work, it directly contradicts the principles behind agile working. The top-down style assumes those at the top have both the knowledge and authority to set OKRs for those further down. Equally it assumes those on the receiving end are indifferent about the origins of goals. Agile thinking questions all such assumptions.

Such a top-down management style is somewhat dated. This approach might have worked in the 1970s, but in the twenty-first century workers expect to have a voice in deciding what work will be done. Enlightened leaders recognize that engaged employees expect to have a voice and that involving them enhances both understanding and motivation.

The rise of digital technology means that any organization adhering to cascading, top-down command-and-control OKRs will not realize the full benefits of digital tools. With machines doing most of the 'heavy lifting', the primary added value of humans is in value judgements and decision-making. When employees are disempowered and must consult 'higher ups' for decisions, the full benefits of digitization cannot be realized.

Rather than thinking of OKRs cascading down from above, think of OKRs cascading up from the teams. One might imagine a CEO with just one objective of their own: *All teams succeed in their goals.*

Leaders are keepers of the company purpose and culture. They are also the highest authority, and must ultimately decide where resources are deployed. Having decided on strategy for furthering purpose and culture, such leaders must decide on missions and the resources available for each mission. Once the stage is set the leaders ask the teams for help.

Before each OKR cycle leaders look to the teams and ask "What can you do to help fulfil our missions, further the company purpose and make the world a better place?".

Teams have specialist skills, knowledge and capabilities. Some provide services, others build products. Some teams are responsible for an entire product or service. At other times multiple teams work together on a bigger thing.

Each hears the leaders' request and listen to the aims and strategy they expound. Equally each team looks at the demands from customers and peer teams and considers the things that need to be done. They then craft OKRs to balance these competing demands.

OKRs are a reply to the leaders' request for help. They follow a common format so that they can be shared, widely understood and compared. At each cycle the OKRs are revisited and reset. A team might find that in one cycle it must prioritize customer needs over company strategy, while the reverse might be true in the next cycle.

As leaders will review the OKRs and – hopefully – provide feedback, they are able to ask "Why?". This process means teams might expose omissions in the leaders' thinking, or provide information leaders were unaware of. This two-way handshake allows OKRs to function as an 'strategy debugger'.

23.5 Summary

- Managers are appointed leaders, but some are better leaders than others. Unofficial leaders can and do emerge.
- Leaders need to set the context of work through culture, big goals and strategy elements.
- Leaders need to embody and live the culture as role models for teams.
- Leaders can promote behaviours and decisions in line with the culture they wish to create simply by saying "Thank you", praising good work and acknowledging effort. Verbal praise can be enhanced with occasional surprise rewards.
- It is the myriad of tiny daily decisions that managers make that bring culture, goals and strategy into being.
- When combined with agile, OKR-setting is more bottom-up than top-down. This allows them to function as *strategy debuggers* and expose misunderstandings and missing information.

24. Culture

*The culture of an organization may be difficult to establish, and to improve –
that can take years, if ever – but it can be easily destroyed given a neglectful
management.*

Henry Mintzberg, *Simply Managing*, 2013

Sustaining OKRs and achieving goals requires a supportive culture. Creating and then sustaining that culture is a large part of leaders' work.

I can't tell you what your culture should be, I can't tell you what the balance between work and play should be, how many fuzzball tables your company should own, which rooms should have beanbags or whether people should bring dogs into the office. I can't even tell you exactly what a corporate culture is – but I can suggest the attributes your culture and your leaders should value and promote to succeed with agile and OKRs.

One might think of these attributes as a balanced Jenga tower: each element supports another layer, and if one element gets removed the whole tower will fall. Unlike a Jenga tower, though, teams move forward. For that to happen individuals and teams need to have ambition, so the metaphor isn't perfect.

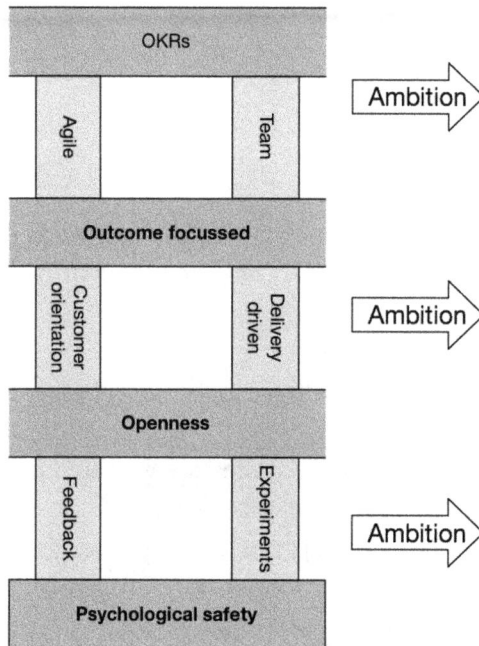

Culture is like a finely balanced Jenga tower, but with motion added by ambition

24.1 Delivery culture

First and foremost your culture needs to value delivery. Not hours worked, not partially done work, not even delivery to user acceptance testing. Delivery means actual working products being used by actual customers.

One of the reasons why agile and OKRs are a good fit is that both aim to create a delivery culture. Anyone considering implementing either agile or OKRs, let alone both, needs to be aiming for leadership and culture that delivers business-beneficial outcomes. Outcomes, not plans.

Although planning is essential, it is only a means to an end. Planning is learning and has its own value, but few customers want to buy a plan: they want to buy an outcome. The rise of digital technology means that today it is often quicker and easier to build something than it is to plan to build it.

Teams are the primary delivery mechanism for agile. OKRs can be very effective when used with teams. So the culture and norms of an organization needs to be team-centric. Teams should not be static, but they should be stable and they should be long-lived. Rather than talk about teams at length I refer readers to my earlier *Xanpan* and *Continuous Digital* books, plus the work of Kazuo Inamori, *Amoeba Management*.

24.2 Customers

Delivery alone is not enough: it doesn't matter what gets delivered if it doesn't provide benefit to someone. That someone is usually a customer who receives the outcomes. It's customers who benefit from the team's creations, therefore it is customers who ultimately determine how much benefit – value – the team has delivered.

However, only delivering benefit to customers is shortsighted: teams need to invest in their own learning and work to improve their productive capacity. But if a team only produces outputs that enhance its ability to deliver, then the sum quantity delivered is zero.

Customers outside the team need to see more than promises of more benefit tomorrow. If nobody outside the team sees benefit, then nobody outside the team will fund further work. A team that managed to fund itself by delivering benefit to itself would be the business equivalent of a perpetual-motion machine.

To deliver customer benefit it is not enough to just deliver *something*. The team must know what customers value, what will bring them benefit. Knowing what a customer will pay for a particular outcome is a good indicator of benefit. Customers will only pay for what they find useful, what makes their lives better, easier or more enjoyable, or allows them to deliver more benefit for less effort to their own customers.

Teams need to know their customers, or at least who the customers should be, to understand what their customers need and what will benefit them. Teams therefore need to be customer-oriented and develop a deep level of customer understanding.

This is easy to see when customers are outside the organization, when they have a choice of the tools they use and when money explicitly changes hands. It is less easy to see when customers are captive within the same organization: the need to think about customer needs and how benefits accrue is even more important precisely because it is harder to see and easier to lose focus.

24.3 Openness and feedback

The short feedback cycles present in both agile and OKRs are there to support feedback and action derived from that feedback. Both implement a version of the Stewart *plan-do-check-act* or Deming *plan-do-study-act* cycle.

For this to work teams need to take an experimental view of each objective. Each, and each key result, is a hypothesis about what will deliver value. Creating each and putting them in front of a customer is an experiment. Equally, undertaking some process improvement is an experiment in what will make the team more productive. Each experiment might succeed and deliver customer benefit.

Some experiments will fail, some hypotheses will be wrong, but each experiment will deliver learning. Learning too has value, for it increases knowledge and informs future actions. Arguably, experiments that fail will produce more learning than those that work.

For a team to maximize learning, therefore, some experiments need to fail. One might think of the 30% of OKRs that are missed as experiments that may have failed, or as OKRs that succeeded in generating learning, provided that the team actively tries to learn from 'failures'.

This in turn means teams and organizations need to be failure-tolerant and not punish people for things that don't work out. Better still, the organization can celebrate failure as a sign that a team is being ambitious and maximizing learning.

One might sum this all up in one word: openness. Organizations, teams and individuals need to be open to new ideas, new thinking, diverse perspectives and alternative views.

24.4 Psychological safety

If teams are to aim high and run experiments, then they and their leaders need to accept that failures will happen – "If you aren't failing, you aren't trying", as someone once said – individuals need *psychological safety*.

Without psychological safety people won't take chances and learning will be inhibited. After all, if we are to learn from failure, we need first to recognize and accept a failure so that learning can begin.

When failure cannot be accepted people will waste a lot of time defending past decisions, arguing that failures were not failures, and finding someone else to blame.

At the most basic level psychological safety means that people do not need to worry that they will lose their jobs when an experiment fails, but it needs to go a lot further than that. People should not fear derision or censure, lost promotion or pay. More positively, individuals need to feel safe to express doubts, ask questions, be honest and be themselves.

Such safety demands that leaders, from the top down, recognize the need for a safe environment. They then need to actually provide that environment, which is easier said than done.

Creating a psychologically safe environment is more about what is not done than what is done: people don't point fingers or apportion blame, people don't take offence when others raise questions and concerns. Leaders play a vital role in modelling the behaviours they want others to follow.

For a full discussion of psychologically safety, see *The Fearless Organization* by Amy C Edmonds, 2019.

24.5 Ambition

Experimentation, failure tolerance, psychological safety and openness provide cultural foundations on which to build agile and OKR success, but alone are not enough.

Individuals and teams need collective ambition to be better at what they do, to learn, to deliver benefit to customers, which implies a desire to learn about customers and their needs. Above all else, they need the ambition to be constantly improving.

While ambition is a powerful motivating force, it is easily lost.

24.6 Summary

- Leaders play an outsized role in establishing, cultivating and sustaining culture within teams and organizations.
- By living the attitudes, behaviours and culture they want to promote, leaders provide a model for others to follow.
- Agile and OKRs both sit well with a culture that values delivering benefit to customers.
- Agile and OKRs support and are supported by similar cultural attributes: customer and outcome orientation, delivery focus, team centricity, failure tolerance and openness.
- Leaders need to recognize the need for psychological safety and work to create a safe environment.
- Just adding OKRs will not make your existing company into a Google.

The next Google?

Perhaps because OKRs have become indelibly associated with Google, and perhaps because so many leaders dream of making their company the next Google, some have come to believe the secret of Google's success *is* OKRs, and that therefore all your company needs to become the next Google is to add OKRs:

Your organization + OKRs = Google

Unfortunately this story is an exaggeration. OKRs are not the only reason Google is successful; there are many other contributing factors. A big part of Google's success is undoubtedly down to the culture Google has created. That culture values delivery and outcomes, and is not scared of experimentation or closing down endeavours that do not deliver hoped-for value.

Undoubtedly Google's early adoption of outcome-focused OKRs helped create that culture and now sustains it. However OKRs were not the only force at work: Google absorbed much of the turn of the millennium Silicon Valley start-up culture, and also absorbed a lot of Stanford graduate school culture.

Perhaps Google adopted OKRs because the culture it was already creating saw OKRs as a good fit. The truth, as always, lies somewhere between the two.

25. Leaders and planning

There is a great deal of talk about loyalty from the bottom to the top. Loyalty from the top down is even more necessary and much less prevalent.

General George S Patton, 1885–1945

In the traditional (pre-agile) world, planning was the responsibility of leadership – or at least of management. There was an implicit belief that leaders planned and workers executed their plans. Once senior brains had made plans, attention shifted to ensuring the plans were followed correctly.

Planning and the plans produced were an intrinsic part of command and control, because a) they showed what was being commanded, and b) they provided a control mechanism. But what freedom of action does anyone have if their future has been planned and programmed?

In the agile world that thinking is inverted. The underlying assumption is that those doing the work are best placed to plan and deliver, using devolved authority and self-organization. The act of planning moves from a chosen few to the wider team, who plan each sprint, update plans in daily stand-ups and, with OKRs, review and replan every quarter.

Which begs the question: *what is a leader's role in planning?*

Even if leaders are no longer planning, they are still held responsible by their superiors and shareholders for future directions.

25.1 Broad–narrow

The answer is a modified version of the *think broad, execute narrow* approach outlined earlier. In the first instance a leader needs to paint the big picture, set the big goals and frame planning discussions.

Unlike teams, which can iterate over weeks between broad thinking and narrow execution, leaders need to switch constantly between re-evaluating the broad approach and supporting narrow delivery.

This might sound nebulous compared to their previous planning role. It is hard to know exactly how one should 'paint the big picture'. It certainly involves lots of speeches, both to groups and one-on-one, maybe pictures or presentations. It is also embedded in the hundreds of decisions a leader makes each day.

Some of those decisions are big: strategy elements, budgets, hire and fire. Many more will be too small to notice: what time to arrive in the morning, which emails to answer immediately and which to postpone, who to give time to, how much time to spend with customers, which teams to visit, where to eat lunch and with whom.

It is leaders' decisions and their behaviour that set the culture and bring strategy to life. It is also in these decisions that leaders focus teams on narrow execution: ultimately, a leader is there to support the teams in delivering.

While individual teams can iterate between one week of broad thinking to set OKRs, then 12 weeks of narrow execution, leaders need to be continually working to expound the broad view. But at the same time, they need to support narrow execution.

Leaders' thinking needs to be ahead of the teams and making sense of the environment. Even as leaders are supporting and enthusing teams, they need to be scanning for new information that might disrupt their plans and efforts.

If a leadership team is to have its own OKRs, it makes sense to set these after delivery teams have agreed theirs. For a leadership team, a recurring objective is helping delivery teams to achieve their OKRs and create benefit.

25.2 Forward planning

When looking to the future – that is, beyond the three-month OKR cycle – culture, big goals and strategy elements play an important role. One cannot know the future, but one can have ambitions for it. One can plan and prepare for the future, but excessive preparation for tomorrow means nothing happens today. Since planning has rapidly diminishing returns, too much planning too early can be counterproductive.

Within these three elements, leaders have a responsibility to describe what the future can be – that is, paint a picture – and where the organization wants to go. Too much detail can be self-defeating: leaders need to set a direction, enthuse people and describe a better world, but also leave space for teams and individuals to fill in the blanks and decide how to get there.

If there is too much detail and no space, there is no scope for individuals and teams to make their own story. No 'white space' means no space for teams to make their own, no space to imagine, no space to interpret, no space to create solutions and no freedom.

While forward planning is primarily driven by the big goals an organization is pursuing, strategy elements are also important. In the short term such elements are largely fixed, while in the longer term they are are malleable.

So, while leaders shouldn't be telling teams what to do, they should be explicitly setting out the big goals for the organization. Next they should give teams enough information to decide for themselves how they can support and deliver those wider organizational goals. To quote General George S Patton again:

> *Never tell people how to do things. Tell them what to do, and they will surprise you with their ingenuity.*

25.3 Cascade up, not down

One of the problems with traditional management by objective is that it becomes a top-down process. Those at the top set objectives that are passed down the line. At each level senior managers refine the MBOs for their department, then cascade them down further.

In contrast, OKRs strive to involve everyone. If they don't – if OKRs are used in a top-down fashion – they are little more than MBOs. If everyone is to truly have a voice, they need to be free to choose their own goals without constraints from above.

So there is a problem: *if leaders are to set direction and the big goals, how are they to communicate this without setting objectives?*

The solution is in two parts:

- First, leaders need to describe their goals, set the vision, paint a picture and inspire people. Leaders need to communicate broadly about big goals while leaving space for others to work out the details. They need to stop short of setting objectives or key results: it is up to teams to do that.
- Second, informed by their leaders, teams need to ask themselves the following questions: *In the next quarter, how can I contribute towards these goals? How can I help our team move towards that goal?*

Thus, while big goals pass down the hierarchy, OKRs should *cascade up rather than down*. Leaders in a hierarchy have a responsibility to those below them to help them deliver their goals. If a leader has individual OKRs, then Objective #1 should be 'My teams succeed in their goals'.

Consider OKR-setting a leadership test: if a leader has described the big goal(s) well enough, then when OKRs trickle up, they should clearly contribute to that goal.

Think of it as the leader setting out the big organizational goals and then asking the teams "How can you help?". Teams reply with OKRs every few months.

Teams need to set OKRs that address the requests from leadership but also address local concerns: requests from other teams, customer feedback, technical challenges and even competitors. Setting OKRs should be neither the top telling the bottom or the bottom telling the top. It should be a shared, collaborative conversation, possibly iterative, to find the goals everyone agrees on.

Orbiting satellites

Organizational charts are inevitably hierarchical and show a top and a bottom, so it becomes natural to frame discussion in terms of messages going up and down the hierarchy. In the twenty first century knowledge economy that model is somewhat dated.

Instead think of electrons racing around the atomic nucleus. Or planets orbiting the Sun. The centre exerts a force which keeps the bodies in orbit but each is independent and different. Those close to the centre feel the force more strongly.

So it is in organizations. The leadership team, the CEO specifically, is at the centre and their decisions, actions and opinions exert a force on teams in orbit. But those teams have their own, local, considerations: customer, competitors, opportunities, threats and other teams. Each team must decide how to act with respect to the forces of both the centre and local area.

25.4 Summary

- Teams, not leaders, plan. Leaders frame the planning discussions through big goals, culture and strategy.
- Leaders can also benefit from iterating between broad and narrow views, however their cycles are likely measured in days or hours rather than weeks.
- Leaders need to leave white space for teams to create their own solutions and innovations.
- OKRs should cascade up, not down.

V Forewarnings

It is impossible to live without failing at something, unless you live so cautiously that you might as well not have lived at all – in which case, you fail by default.

J K Rowling, author

26. Aspirations

Our problem is not that we aim too high and miss, but that we aim too low and hit.

Variously attributed to Artistotle, American motivational speaker Les Brown and others

Most of the accounts of OKRs emphasize their aspirational nature. While the aspirational attributes of OKRs are highly desirable, there is significant value in using OKRs even if your aspirations are a little more mundane.

Used in *aspirational mode* OKRs are 'moonshots'. OKRs motivate teams to achieve '10x' (that's *ten times* to most of us) performance. It could be 10x team effectiveness, 10x product impact or both. In aspirational mode OKRs aim higher than the team believes it can achieve. The organization accepts that OKRs will be missed, that teams will *fail*. In fact, teams are *expected* to fail their OKRs.

The underlying assumption is that a team aiming to achieve a tenfold improvement – say boosting website views from 1,000 a day to 10,000 a day – may miss its target. But in aiming ridiculously high, the team will outperform a more modest team that aims low and achieves its goal.

Failing to meet a tenfold improvement target – say achieving 5,000 views per day – will still be a greater improvement than a team that plays safe. A team that is playing safe may aim for a 10% improvement – say to raise views per day from 1,000 to 1,100 – and may well meet its goal.

The outcome-oriented nature of OKRs implicitly recognizes that labels like 'success' and 'failure' are less important than the result achieved. There is however a conflict hidden in this approach: a 'failure' can be a better result than a 'success'. This can create cognitive dissonance for both team members and those managing such teams.

An outcome can have both success ("We raised website views five-fold!") and failure ("We missed our OKR!"). As is often the case, the labels *success* and *failure* are applied after the event and depend on perspective. On the face of it OKRs are objective (you hit or miss) but subjectivity is never far away.

26.1 Utility mode

Alternatively the OKR mechanism can be used in *utility mode*. Even without 10x aspirations there are still benefits from having shared team OKRs. These have already been outlined, but are with repeating:

- Promoting an outcome orientation and business benefit.
- Prioritizing work to be done.
- Increasing focus by de-prioritizing potential work, thereby allowing focus on remaining work.
- Sharing goals across the team.
- Communicating team goals to the wider organization.
- Providing medium-term planning.
- Clarifying targets and objectives.
- Creating context for technical and business decisions.

Even without aspirations OKRs have plenty to offer. There is benefit in using OKRs even when used in a conservative utility mode. For those adopting OKRs for the first time, this approach sidesteps several potential pitfalls.

26.2 Predictability

Aiming high and accepting 'failure' sounds good and aspirational. But organizations value predictability; aiming high and accepting that you might miss doesn't sit well with those who want certainty. I remember one set of stakeholders who became agitated when told a team only expected to achieve 70% of planned OKRs.

Utility mode OKRs can help here too. Aiming high when stakeholders and the organization value predictability is probably not a good tactic. As a tool OKRs can still help and still deliver benefits. You might want to rate each OKR on a scale of 1 to 10, where 1 is unlikely and 10 very likely. Show your stakeholders, and if they are unhappy rework the OKRs so that they fit an acceptable risk profile.

To complicate matters, unfortunately organizations and even individuals are not always consistent. While one leader advocates aspirational OKRs, and even claims to accept failure, others might demand certainty. In such cases you might want to bring divergent thinkers together and outline the mismatch.

26.3 Creating aspirations?

It would be naive to claim that adding OKRs to any team will miraculously turn it into a high-performing aspirational one. Naturally I would love it if this were the case, but 'just add OKRs' is not as simple as 'just add water'.

OKRs are certainly one tool for nudging a team towards higher performance and greater aspiration, but they are not enough on their own. Promoting high performance and aspiration requires a supportive environment and culture – in other words, *psychological safety* (discussed earlier).

Many accounts of OKRs focus on the aspirational nature of OKRs in Google and Intel. As such these accounts say much about the culture and approach of highly successful companies. Entire books have been written about these companies and how they foster such a culture, so I will only point out a few elements:

- A 'safe to fail' environment.
- Motivated individuals.
- Opportunity and a resource-rich environment, with a willingness to let motivated individuals fail.
- Evaluation and reward systems that recognize failures as being equivalent to successes.

Even Google and Intel will fail on some of these points – and those who know these companies from the inside may see more inconsistencies. But even as they fail on some points, they succeed on enough points to perpetuate a culture that values aspiration.

Once a company has such a culture the whole thing becomes self-perpetuating (indeed, all cultures tend to become self-perpetuating, for better or for worse). Individuals who value these attributes will want to work at such places, while those who don't share their values will go elsewhere. Peer pressure and individuals' desire to fit in will become self-reinforcing.

26.4 Leaders and culture

For companies that want to adopt aspects of aspirational culture – what might be called *Silicon Valley culture* – there are formidable obstacles. OKRs may well form part of that change, but they are not alone.

In particular, companies need to recognize that the people they employ are, almost by definition, different to people who work in companies with an aspirational culture. The existing company culture will have already filtered out some of these aspirational individuals.

Those who are employed have proved themselves compatible with the existing culture; that culture will have rewarded them for working within it and punished them for not doing so. Over time it will filter out people who are incompatible. Switching to an aspirational culture takes more than flipping the 'OKR light switch'.

Company leaders usually recognize this, but often fail to comprehend how their own actions are seen. A leader can stand on stage and tell their workforce passionately about the change they want to see, they can articulate OKRs in detail, and they can truly believe what they say. But workers have often seen this before: company change programmes come along regularly. Leaders frequently want to change something. Workers are almost programmed to be cynical.

As a result workers listen and watch. They look to see if the leader is *walking the walk* or just *talking the talk*. The cynical amongst them believe it is all 'management talk'. Any action the leader takes – any displeasure they voice, any incongruent set of actions, let alone anger or punishment meted out – will quickly be seized on as proof that they do not mean what they say.

26.5 An OKR adoption route

If you work in a high-performing aspirational company, then great. Adopt OKRs and everything will be even better.

For everyone else, let me make a suggestion.

Aspire to aspirational OKRs, but make the change in small steps.

A psychologically safe environment is critical for aspirational OKRs to work. So do a quick assessment, and if you are anything less than 100% sure, start the conversation about what is needed and ask for help. If your objective is success with OKRs, then the first key result is a boost in psychological safety.

Start by using OKRs in *utility mode*. Better still, perform the exercise I describe next; you might find you are not quite as 'utility mode' as you think. But wherever you start, just start.

Start setting OKRs on a regular basis. Work towards them and get better at setting and delivering against your OKRs. Inject safety into the system before teams are ready to use it, so that they can 'take up the slack' when they are ready. With time the team may be willing to take on more risk and be more aspirational.

While the team is perfecting its use of utility-mode OKRs, work on the rest of the company. My guess is that if you are adopting OKRs, you are not alone. Other teams may be adopting them, while more senior people in the company may want them to be adopted. Work with the grain and nudge these people in the right direction.

As you do so, the problems of using OKRs in an unfriendly environment will become clearer. Work on these issues. Use OKRs as a problem detector to find out what needs to be changed. Don't work alone, work with others who are adopting OKRs to nudge people and the organization in the right direction.

Work on yourself: indeed work to change yourself more than anyone else. Keep an eye on your language: 'success' and 'failure' are loaded terms. Make sure your actions fit with your talk: you are a leader too and you also need to 'walk the walk'.

Involve your personnel and human resources staff: ask them to observe your OKR-setting and ask for their thoughts. Show them the outcomes: working software. Keep talking to them.

Above all else you need to work out how OKRs relate to your performance appraisal programmes and salary reviews. The simplest advice is to keep OKRs separate from these annual checkpoints, but no organization seems to follow this advice.

Progress to conversation with your superiors and the people to which the team answers. Some discussions are better held in the open with other team members, while others are better held in private with superiors.

This isn't a comprehensive list of suggestions, it isn't even a long list, but it is a starting point.

26.6 Exercise: where are you?

Imagine a line of numbers from one to ten. At one end 'one' is labelled *utility mode*. Here OKRs are used for team cohesion, shared understanding and medium-term planning. Achieving the objectives and key results is important.

The other end of the line, 'ten', is labelled *aspirational mode*. At this end teams are stretching themselves, aiming for 10x solutions and shooting for the moon. The team, those around them, and importantly management, recognize that OKRs may be hit or missed. The real evaluation is the outcome of the work of the team.

Utility mode ←——————————————————————→ Aspirational mode

1   2   3   4   5   6   7   8   9   10

OKRs set based on what is achievable   Moonshot OKRs set based aspiration
Predictability is valued   Impact is valued
Teams aim to achieve all OKRs   Teams expect to fail stretch OKRs

Utility mode is one end of the spectrum, aspirational mode is the other

All ten points on this spectrum are respectable places to be. Each position represents a legitimate way of working.

Ask yourself: *where would you put your team on this spectrum?*

The position you choose will naturally reflect your own ambitions and aspirations. It will also reflect the environment you work in: high-risk high-reward start-up or low-risk modest-reward legacy bank.

Knowing your appetite for risk will help you when setting OKRs.

More importantly, you will want to agree this position with your team. After all, the whole team is signing up to a set of OKRs, so it is important that the whole team understands the context. Don't impose your position on the team, so ask members where they think the team should aim.

Start by drawing the line on a board. Mark it 1 to 10 and talk about what each extreme implies. Then have every team member write down the number that reflects the position they think the team should occupy. Wait till everyone has written down their own private number, put the papers in a pile and shuffle them to keep answers anonymous. Then mark the numbers on the 1 to 10 line.

Discuss the results. Maybe the whole team agrees, which is great. If not, ask why some people might vote low and some high. Work through the reasoning and decide on a shared position.

26.7 Summary

- Advocates of OKRs usually emphasize their aspirational nature. While aspirational OKRs can be immensely powerful, they only work when the organization has a compatible culture and provides psychological safety.
- The other benefits of OKRs justify using them in utility mode: to create focus around shared priorities, promote medium-term planning, communicate direction and more. Such utility OKRs can have benefits even if it is only your team using them.
- OKRs can help where a company is attempting to transition to a more aspirational culture. However they are not enough on their own. More needs to change to make the organization and culture aspirational.

27. Everyday pitfalls

As a rule, software systems do not work well until they have been used, and have failed repeatedly, in real applications.

Dave Parnas, Professor of Computer Science

As with software, so with processes and OKRs. Until a team has tried using OKRs and debugged their own process, it will not work well. Many of those pitfalls – bugs – arise from a need to find a balance between opposing forces.

Combining OKRs with agile offers the chance to find a balance between those forces: between devolved and centralized authority, between pursuing one's aims and responding to change, and between succeeding through determination – staying the course – and seizing the opportunities presented by change.

One should see OKRs as permission-givers rather than shackles. For an agile team OKRs should be carving out space for autonomy and space to fail. Those failures will include failure to achieve objectives and key results, and failures in setting and using OKRs.

The team's autonomy in setting goals and agreeing them with others, senior managers included, makes space for teams to excel. But that does not mean OKRs are easy, either to set or to deliver. Nor does it mean that they are obvious. Teams will take several iterations to learn how to make them work, and since each iteration typically takes three months, that will feel like a long time.

OKRs are deceptively simple: decide what you want to achieve and set out how it will be measured. But, in setting OKRs, executing against OKRs and evaluating the results, there are many things that can go wrong. Some of the pitfalls have already been discussed. In this chapter and those that follow I will highlight several more.

27.1 'OKR buffet'

An 'OKR buffet' is a particular example of failure by having too many OKRs. When teams have too many OKRs team members can feel at liberty to choose which OKRs they want to pursue.

In such cases individuals may focus, but teams don't pull together and achieve larger OKRs. The team may achieve several small objectives, or it may fail completely.

OKR buffets happen when teams don't face up to hard decisions while setting OKRs. Instead set OKRs that include 'something for everyone'. This is particularly true when each team member wants their own OKR.

If each team member truly has different skills, different aims and different goals, then the team isn't a team. If there is nothing to unite around then it isn't a team: it is a group of individuals who are bunched together. In effect, each person is a team of one with their own OKR(s) to pursue.

27.2 Late-arriving OKRs

Late-arriving OKRs are another problem to watch for. At a late stage one team member will add extra OKRs to the draft list. Usually this becomes apparent when a team member shows their proposed OKRs to others and the team member says "I added this extra one to cover..."

Needless to say, late additions are best avoided. Creating OKRs in a rush risks compressing discussion or skipping it altogether; time is not allowed for others to comment. Creating OKRs is an opportunity to enrol team members in a collective endeavour, so don't delegate writing to just one or two people.

Without team enrollment OKRs are more difficult to achieve. More problematically, such OKRs dilute focus on other OKRs and lead to an OKR buffet. Late-arriving OKRs may be a sign that team members don't feel part of the team and actively desire an objective for themselves.

27.3 Adding to the story hierarchy

Most agile teams use user stories for requirements and backlogs. With stories come epics and tasks: the three form a hierarchy. Those well-versed in this mental model frequently jump to adding objectives and key results to the hierarchy:

- Objectives break down to key results.
- Key results break down to epics.
- Epics break down to stories.
- Stories break down to tasks.

- Tasks are the work to be done.

Avoid the temptation to do this. Five levels of hierarchy is too many, and poses an administrative nightmare. Three levels can model just about anything: see *Little Book of User Stories*[^Kelly2017−2] for more discussion.

Secondly, this hierarchy implies size and value:

- Objectives are bigger than key results.
- Key results are bigger than epics.
- Epics are bigger than stories.
- Stories are bigger than tasks.

This hierarchy does not always hold: a key result might be one story, or even just a few tasks. In assuming this hierarchy, future discussions over effort estimates and value estimates are already framed with unproven assumptions.

Work with the OKRs directly. Every time you need to think about what to do next, ask:

- Is this objective achieved?
- If not, are all key result achieved?
- If not, then what needs to be done next to move forward?

When you understand what needs to be done, decide whether that would be a task, a story or an epic in your setup.

Rather than seeing a hierarchy of objectives, key results, epics and stories, see OKRs as the reason for writing and doing stories. Use OKRs as an engine to create stories just in time – that is, just before they are worked on.

27.4 Counting problems

In order to meet an objective and count it as done, *do you need to meet all the key results?*

What if, having written and agreed an OKR, the team discovers a way of realizing the objective without achieving any of the key results? Or what if they achieve one key result of three, or two?

There may be no definite answer to these questions. For some objectives the key results may be little more than a plan of action. If you find a better route to achieve that objective, then *who cares about the key results?*

Conversely, some objectives may be the sum of the key results: achieving two key results may satisfy 60% of the objective, but what of the last result and the other 40%?

How you count OKRs may seem obvious when you first look, but once you start on actual work it can become less clear. While one can strive for objectives and results, *the devil is in the detail*: what appears obvious at first may be far from obvious once one understands the details.

Of course it would be nice to iron out all these quirks in advance, but no matter how carefully one sets OKRs, anomalies will arise. Exhaustive up-front analysis can be time-consuming; rather than paralysis-by-analysis, it is better to start work with the imperfect and see what happens.

27.5 Respect for specialists

While team members share the responsibility for setting OKRs, they need to respect others: specialists, customers and those the organization places in positions of authority. Failing to respect and listen to others may result in self-serving OKRs that nobody outside the team values.

When setting OKRs all team members have a voice, but that does not mean all team members are equal. It is likely that most OKRs will address business problems, opportunities in the market and customer needs.

On an agile team there is usually at least one team member who specializes in these issues. This is the Product Owner, often assisted by business analysts and product managers, who work within or alongside the team. Since the Product Owner is a specialist in what others need and where the team can add value, it is likely that they will take the lead in OKR-setting.

Conversely, when OKRs are technically oriented, it makes sense for the specialists in that area have a leading say. Say the team wants to experiment with using a new JavaScript library, then it is sensible for JavaScript specialists to say more than the Product Owner.

Each team member brings specialist skills and knowledge; this gives them more authority in some areas, but equally reduces their authority in others. Team members need to respect each others' authority in specific areas.

27.6 Respect for managers

No team is an island, and each must listen to what customers and other stakeholders want, need and expect. Some of those people will have more influence than others, such as major customers who write large cheques.

Yet there is one group of stakeholders some in the agile community shun: managers. The ethos of self-organizing and self-managing teams is sometimes taken to mean *no managers*. That may on occasion be true: while manager-free teams exist, most teams answer to managers at some level.

Authoritarian managers are clearly a bad fit with agile teams, but not all managers are authoritarians. Managers have specialist skills too: business, coordination, administration, communication and more. Managers are stakeholders; some managers are team members, others are involved third parties.

Managers, executives, directors and others in positions of responsibility are representatives of the company owners, and as such they have a right to be heard and their opinions respected. In many organizations these people will also be the gatekeepers of additional resources and influence.

Agile working encourages teams to self-organize and maybe even self-manage, but that does not mean they have a licence to do as they like. Most teams need to explain themselves to others.

Both sides – teams and managers – need to find a balance: a balance between the decentralized authority of the team and the centralized authority of managers. Neither side has the right to decide OKRs alone, but neither does either side to have the right to force OKRs on the other.

Forcing OKRs onto a team is a sure way of destroying motivation, responsibility and engagement. Forcing OKRs onto managers will poison a relationship and store up problems for later.

27.7 Summary

Potential OKR pitfalls can include:

- Having too many OKRs.
- OKRs added late in the setting process without the same amount of discussion and refinement as others.
- Failure to focus on OKRs and the discipline to stay focused.
- Having an 'OKR buffet' with objectives for team members to choose from and little shared focus.
- Untestable key results.
- Not having a strategy for business as usual and consequently being derailed by it.
- Bolting OKRs into the agile work hierarchy of epics, stories and tasks.
- Ambiguity around counting OKR success.
- Lack of respect for specialists, external stakeholders and, in particular, managers.

28. Trouble with targets

The Gross National Product does not include the beauty of our poetry or the intelligence of our public debate. It measures neither our wit nor our courage, neither our wisdom nor our learning, neither our compassion nor our devotion. It measures everything, in short, except that which makes life worthwhile.

Robert Kennedy, US politician, 1925–1968

If one is looking for a reason to discredit OKRs, look no further: this chapter makes an excellent starting point. Conversely, anyone promoting OKRs should understand the opposing arguments. It is for you to choose how you want to answer these critiques.

This book, along with much of the writing on OKRs, and indeed management writing as a whole, advocates explicit goals, the quantification of those goals and the measurement of progress. I believe such practices increase focus and therefore improve effectiveness.

However, I also acknowledge that reducing everything to a number is an oversimplification. Focus can lead to a blinkered view, and chasing goals risks unintended consequences.

Obviously these two views pull in different directions. Both are valid arguments, and both extremes are wrong – the truth lies somewhere in the middle.

Such problems and indeed this whole chapter may seem irrelevant to the day-to-day use of OKRs. However, these issues are insidious; over time they will detract from the efficacy of OKRs. The first step towards avoiding them is awareness.

Ultimately there may be no solution to such differences; instead one must learn to balance between the two opposing forces. Walking this tightrope is an ongoing balancing act that demands respect for both sides.

28.1 Targeting the measurable

As the opening quote highlights, there are things that might not be measurable. While there have been attempts to measure happiness, and at least one body produces a world happiness report[1], how many of us actively quantify our happiness? How many of us target our happiness year-on-year? Are those who do quantify their happiness actually happier than those who don't? And how can one tell?

Indeed, one can even argue that the most important decisions we make in life – whether to marry, who to marry, how many children to have, which house to buy, which jobs to accept and which to reject, and who to include in our will – get made not on data but on emotion, feelings and intuition.

Some of this might be laziness, after all; such quantification is hard and many of us lack the necessary skills. Earlier I give suggestions about how to measure and quantify targets. I respect Tom Gilb when he says he can measure love with a number – although I have never had a chance to ask his wife's view of this measurement.

28.2 Questions measurement can't answer

Even if one wants to measure everything and make data-driven choices, can one afford the cost? Consider a manager who finds the need to arbitrate in a conflict between two employees. Would they have the time to measure the conflict? Model the potential outcome and make a data-driven decision?

Even if they had time to do this, who would see the decision as fair and legitimate? Suppose they conclude that one employee should be let go as a result of the conflict. A rational decision might be that while Sasha is in the wrong, Alex is the one to fire, because Sasha is more productive. How would other employees see this decision?

The manager could revisit their model and could factor in the effects on other employees. *How disgruntled would they be? How much would productivity change? What effect might the decision make on staff retention?*

The model would grow and grow. The time needed to research the answer would grow, and while the manager might have a defensible position, would it satisfy others? *Does rationality sit well with fairness?* Maybe it would for a perfectly rational human – the so called *homo economicus*, economic man – but would it for you?

28.3 Goodhart's Law

Goodhart's Law[2]: 'When a measure becomes a target, it ceases to be a good

---

[1]https://worldhappiness.report/
[2]https://en.wikipedia.org/wiki/Goodhart%27s_law

measure.' Charles Goodhart, professor of economics

Charles Goodhart coined his eponymous law in the 1970s while discussing government attempts to reduce inflation by targeting money supply – the amount of money in the economy. As the British Government tried to reduce inflation by reducing the money supply, the behaviour of money – or rather the behaviour of people using money – changed. Rather than cash, people could use cheques or credit cards; rather than put savings in a bank, they could use a non-bank building society. Over time it became increasingly difficult to even define what money is, something that is even more difficult in the age of bitcoin and digital money.

Similar phenomenon are seen elsewhere in society, for example hospitals chasing targets that adopt behaviours that meet the target but do not contribute to patient wellbeing, or train companies that extend journey times to meet punctuality targets.

Nor was Goodhart the only one to observe this phenomenon. Psychologist Donald T Cambell coined his own law:

> Campbell's law[3]: 'The more any quantitative social indicator is used for social decision-making, the more subject it will be to corruption pressures and the more apt it will be to distort and corrupt the social processes it is intended to monitor.'
> Donald T Campbell, social scientist

The most obvious example in software development is *velocity*, the popular mechanism agile teams use to track progress and make forecasts. I have seen teams where velocity only ever increased: at every sprint the team delivered more velocity points than ever before. Yet the amount of software functionality or capabilities didn't keep pace.

Consciously or subconsciously, team members 'devalue' velocity points: estimates get bigger, so while the final number is larger, it represents less. That is what economists call *inflation*. It would be naive to think OKRs would somehow be exempt from such effects.

That might be a reason for changing measurements frequently. It also serves to emphasize the importance of ensuring that everyone understands why a target exists and that everyone agrees on how to measure it.

Explicit objectives and targets are good, because they set a course and serve as a guide to future decisions, enhance shared understanding and team working, promote focus and help demonstrate progress. But having a target without understanding risks hitting the target but missing the goal. Quantitive targets need to be combined with qualitative understanding.

---

[3]https://en.wikipedia.org/wiki/Campbell%27s_law

28.4 Goal displacement

OKRs are good because they create focus – they allow teams to measure progress towards their goal. But sometimes people mistake the measurement for the goal itself, something sociologist Robert K Merton termed *goal displacement*.

For example, if a team target is '10% more visitors to the online shop', it may be that '10%' looms larger in the mind than 'visitors'. There are a number of dubious means that can be used increase the number of visitors that might allow the target to be met while undermining its intention. Black-hat SEO techniques might boost visitor numbers in the short term while damaging them in the long term.

Similarly, focusing on the target and losing the context can lead to a drop in quality. 'Low quality' visitors may meet the target but not its intention.

For example, an OKR that asks a team to 'deliver at least ten user stories per sprint' might simply lead to teams dropping quality standards. Coders and testers could, consciously or subconsciously, overlook defects that would soon be found by customers.

The work involved in logging customer problems, administering remedial work, performing a fix, retesting and releasing a fix will probably be greater than the effort saved with the initial shortcut.

Attentive readers will recognize both these examples as cases of *Goodhart's Law* and *unintended consequences* – another term credited to Robert K Merton.

Goals should be chased and targets should be met, but not at any cost. Teams may challenge norms: they should think of new approaches and try new ideas, but need to be conscious of company norms, culture and boundaries. They should not act maliciously or counter to long-term interests.

Of course there is a judgement call here – *when are you challenging and when are you going too far?* If in doubt, ask – have a conversation. If you find yourself reluctant to tell others about your approach, it may be that you already know it contravenes expected standards.

28.5 Overcoming tunnel vision

While elsewhere I have suggested taking a blinkered view during OKR delivery, one should not push that view too far. Choosing objectives to match what can be measured, pursuing objectives to the detriment of others or focusing exclusively on objectives in the midst of a crisis all represent dangerous tunnel vision.

There are times when it is right to ignore distractions and the chaos that surrounds us in order to focus on our goals. There are also times when ignoring what is happening around us is irresponsible. Unfortunately there is no rule or metric to tell us which path to follow, when to stay the course and when to go off-piste.

Rules of thumb

For a few days a quarter, when setting OKRs, default to expansive thinking – talk broadly and subjectively. Then narrow conversation to create objective OKRs.

While executing OKRs, default to objective thinking: focus on targets and measures.

As with all defaults, sometimes you need to override them.

Such problems will only become worse if organizations sanction team members for not meeting OKRs. That might not be a direct reprimand to one's face – it might be a sarcastic comment, a decision to promote someone with a record of achieving OKRs, a financial bonus not awarded or a smaller pay rise.

Indeed, perceived sanctions – where an employee imagines sanctions when there are none – are probably more dangerous than actual sanctions, because they easily multiply in peoples' minds. Such imagined slights are also more difficult to disprove.

Leaders at all levels need to work hard to counter tunnel vision and perceptions. The difficult part is to balance the wide, unblinkered view with the absolute focus that OKRs need to succeed.

As with so much else, iteration can help: look broadly and subjectively when deciding on OKRs, allow time to think expansively and hear different views. Decide on goals, focus the goals with numbers, then execute with that focus. Accept doubts when executing OKRs but don't jump to change course. When a time-box ends, evaluate the results and return to broad subjective mode to learn lessons and set new OKRs.

Repeat. Iterate. What could be more agile than that?

28.6 A final warning: targets

One doesn't have to go far into history to find examples of targets that lead good people astray. Whether body counts in Vietnam or cross-selling at Wells Fargo, there are plenty of examples of what happens when targets go too far. Pursuing numerical targets for 12 out of 13 weeks is a powerful approach, but it needs to be moderated if the kind of problems described here are to be avoided.

So when goals are reviewed in the final week of the quarter and new ones set, think broadly. Let everyone speak openly and safely, listen to concerns and think again about purpose and mission.

One quarter pursing erroneous targets or one quarter encouraging malevolent practices may be bad, but it usually isn't the end of the world. Be big enough to recognize problems and correct them.

A far bigger mistake is not to recognize problems and to repeat erroneous or misleading targets for another quarter. Or, as agile says: *inspect and adapt.*

28.7 Summary

Having spent most of this book arguing for objective, clear and quantified targets, this chapter highlights the dangers inherent in such targets. Avoiding these dangers starts with awareness. Deliberately iterating between subjective setting and objective execution is one way to balance both sides.

- Complete measurement might not be possible, and even thorough measurement can be time-consuming and costly.
- Even a completely rational and quantified decision may not seem equitable or reasonable to employees, customers or other stakeholders.
- Quantified targets have a bad habit of causing unexpected side effects, *unintended consequences.* It is therefore important to combine both hard quantified targets with a softer understanding of objectives.
- Aim to set objective OKRs while having subjective conversations about them. During execution be objective in focusing on OKRs, but allow your inner voice to raise doubts.

29. Individuals and performance reviews

You cannot hope to build a better world without improving the individuals. To that end each of us must work for his own improvement, and at the same time share a general responsibility for all humanity, our particular duty being to aid those to whom we think we can be most useful.

Marie Curie, physicist, 1867–1934

Let me be as clear as possible:

Don't link renumeration to OKR outcomes.

Don't pay bonuses or offer financial incentives for achieving objectives or key results.

Adding money to OKR outcomes is self-defeating. It changes implicit internal motivation into external motivation. It encourages gaming the system, changes the nature of the metrics you are using and creates unintended consequences.

It's not just me who says this. Every book or blog I've ever read about OKRs, every podcast and experienced speaker I've listened to makes the same point:

> *Divorce compensation (both raises and bonuses) from OKRs. These should be two distinct conversations, with their own cadences and calendars. The first is a backward-looking assessment, typically held at year's end. The second is an ongoing, forward-looking dialog between leaders and contributors.* John Doerr, *Measure What Matters*

Financial incentives might work the first time, they might even work a second time, but by then people are trained and expect rewards. Withdraw them and you destroy the system, keep them and the system will slowly decay back to where it was before.

While I have never, *never* heard anyone advocate linking financial incentives to OKR outcomes, it seems that line managers and 'human resource' departments cannot resist the temptation. After all, who can blame them: performance reviews are hard work, so why not use an existing ready-made quantified measurement?

The performance review problem gets supercharged when money enters the picture. Attaching bonuses and prizes for OKR completion may guarantee that OKRs will be met. It also equally guarantees that Goodhart's Law will play out: people will find ways of meeting the targets. In the process the measurement will become corrupted and unintended consequences created.

Linking individuals' compensation to OKR success will have similar effects: targets will be met at the cost of side effects. Once money is attached to OKRs, people feel compelled to chase 100% success. The easiest way to do this is to set a lower target.

If a target is changed, say to 70% OKR completion, people will simply play a more sophisticated game. Achievable targets will be set and the team will only just over-perform.

When a company values ambition it should make ambition the safe option. When someone has debts to pay off, a mortgage or rent to pay each month, or a family to support, who can blame them for putting ambition second?

29.1 Integrating employee reviews with OKRs

OKRs are usually set quarterly, so it seems logical to conduct employee reviews on the same schedule. Of course one could go further and conduct them monthly or on every sprint, but there is always a balance to be struck between improving work and doing work. For many managers doing any sort of review more often than annually will be a challenge. So start by moving to quarters and then decide what to do next.

John Doerr suggests *CFRs* (conversation, feedback and recognition) as a framework for *continuous performance management*. Since I have no direct experience of CFRs and don't wish to repeat Doerr's, I direct readers to his book and add my own own experiences and suggestions here.

While it may seem obvious to reward people for achieving OKRs, doing so is likely to create unintended and undesirable results. A reward system that rewards people for achieving OKRs will incentivize people to achieve OKRs by whatever means possible, whatever the side effects.

Rather, the goal of OKRs – the goal beyond the goal, if you like – is not 'completed objectives'. The 'goal beyond' is a value-enhancing outcome. OKRs are a Matryoshka inside a Matryoshka – the outer Matryoshka takes priority. Incentives should therefore be at least one level above OKRs.

Since OKRs are the means of delivering the outer Matryoshka, one may also consider an individual's contribution to OKRs and the process itself. That is: don't look at what was delivered against the target, look at how team members contributed to the process of that delivery.

Did the team member contribute to setting the targets? Did they speak their mind? Did they make contributions – perhaps by highlighting potential flaws or by suggesting better metrics?

Were individuals engaged in the delivery process? Did they work as part of the team? Or did they stick to their traditional area of work and follow their own priorities?

Disagree and commit

Jeff Bezos of Amazon[a] has advocated the use of 'disagree and commit'. Seeking consensus on a decision may slow down decision-making and result in a weak option winning through. Far better, says Bezos, for individuals to say "I disagree and commit": while accepting a decision they do not agree with, they are nevertheless prepared to work to towards delivering the goal.

[a]https://www.aboutamazon.com/news/company-news/2016-letter-to-shareholders

---

29.2 OKRs for individuals

My experience concerns OKRs with teams, either teams I am coaching or teams I am part of. As such the OKRs play into organizational OKRs – either creating OKRs that align with or influence enterprise OKRs.

OKRs are a tool to be used with teams – this is the 'OKR sweet spot'. I avoid setting OKRs for individuals. In a team setting any individual goals should contribute to team goals.

When people are working as part of a team having their own individual goals creates a potential conflict. When a team has OKRs, team members should be contributing towards the team OKRs.

So, what if an individual is given OKRs of their own? Either the individual OKRs contribute directly to the team OKRs – in which case, what do individual OKRs add? Alternatively, the OKR is something extra, 'above and beyond' and specific to the team member. In which case, which OKR has priority? *Where should the individual's focus be?*

An individual who is part of a team should be focused on contributing as much as they can to the team. There is only one objective for that individual:

Help the team succeed

Giving individuals their own goals in addition potentially conflicts with the team's objectives. If it does not conflict, then what is the point? If an individual's OKRs are completely aligned with the team's goals, then such OKRs are superfluous and just add to administration.

That said, there may still be cases in which it makes sense to set an individual personal goals. Consider a team that adopts an objective to enhance learning with a key result of 'attend tech talks'. It could then make sense to task each team member with a personal goal of delivering one tech talk themselves.

Or consider the case in which an individual is seeking a different role. Imagine a programmer who aspires to product management. Together with a mentor, they may identify some areas for the individual to work on, perhaps learning about product management or exhibiting certain behaviours.

Both these cases could be pursued without conflicting with team goals even though they are specific to individuals. Still, priorities need to be clear, and 'helping the team succeed' should always be objective #1.

When it comes to individual OKRs, then, my default answer is: don't. Focus on team goals by limiting priorities and enhancing team work.

Behaviours

When considering employee conduct it helps to look at employee behaviour. Behaviours are observable – one can see whether an individual contributes to discussions, whether they move their work tickets across the board or whether they turn every meeting into an opportunity to complain. Behaviours are teachable, behaviours can be modelled and copied, and poor behaviours can be unlearned.

Think about what behaviours you would like from your team members? What kind of behaviour makes work go more smoothly?

Equally, what behaviour gets in the way? What behaviour creates problems? Be careful not to let your own preferences dominate.

Which team members display these behaviours? Simply praising the right behaviours is a good start. You might go further and talk about those behaviours as a team, see if others agree with you, and whether some might adopt similar behaviours.

Equally, you could talk about the not-so-good behaviours, but tread carefully – you don't want to upset people. Rather, understand what might be bringing those behaviours about and what can be changed to improve things.

29.3 Summary

- Do not link financial bonuses with OKRs.
- Do not link OKR achievement to salary, renumeration or any other payment.
- OKRs can, even should, be subject to discussion in employee review sessions. Do not judge employees on progress, success or failure of an OKR itself, rather consider how the employee works with OKRs.
- Individual OKRs may or may not be useful; if used, they should not detract from the individual's role in helping their team achieve collective goals.

Close

Closing words

What I'm proposing, to myself and other people, is what I often call the tourist attitude – that you act as though you've never been there before. So that you're not supposed to know anything about it. If you really get down to brass tacks, we have never been anywhere before.

John Cage, composer, 1912–1992

The first edition of this book attempted to share what I learned during a year working with agile teams and OKRs. Maybe if I had waited until I had two years' experience I would have more and better advice to give, but I wanted to write it now while all these learnings are fresh in my head and before I lose that all-important *tourist mentality*. This is the book I wish I had had when I began the OKR journey. The second edition refine those learnings and shares a few more.

If you had told me a few years ago that I would write a book about OKRs I would not have believed you. I was skeptical about OKRs; they sounded like a reinvention of MBOs – management by objective – with a similar set of associated problems plus a quantification fetish. Catch me in a pompous mood and I will readily claim credit for introducing the software industry to *Goodhart's Law*.

So when I learned the organization I was helping to become agile was also introducing OKRs I was armed with plenty of arguments – but I bit my tongue. Sometimes one has to pick one's battles – or at least pick the right time to fight.

After a little consideration I decided to see the introduction of OKRs not as a problem, not as something to fight, but as an opportunity. Working with OKRs could be a great experiment – do they work? Are my fears well-founded? If nothing else, it helps to *know thy enemy*.

Over the months of working with OKRs, helping two teams set and pursue them directly, plus being a member of a third team writing and pursuing OKRs, I had the opportunity to discuss OKRs with my fellow agile coaches, and my opinion changed.

As Nietzsche wrote, *'What does not kill me makes me stronger'*. After working with OKRs intensively for a year I still had my doubts, but I could see how they work, and work well. Indeed, more than that, I see great promise in OKRs. I need to run some more experiments.

I wanted to capture this learning for myself, but, as every author knows, the person who learns most from a book is the person who writes the book. Writing a book forces one to distill one's thinking and reconcile one's logic. Hopefully readers will learn too, but the process of capturing, structuring and communicating one's thoughts leads to more and deeper insights.

More than this, though, writing a book forces you to explore where your thinking goes. For example, in writing the strategy and planning chapters here, I had to do more than draw on direct experience: I had to extend my thinking to work out how the different moving parts of agile, OKRs, strategy and planning all interlocked.

So thank you, dear reader – thank you for helping me to learn. I hope I can help you too.

Would I recommend OKRs to a friend? Yes.

Would I introduce OKRs to a team and an organization? Yes.

Do I continue to harbor reservations? Yes again.

Like so many other tools, OKRs can be used for good or for bad. They can be used in better ways and worse ways. They are far from foolproof, but I believe they have a place.

Get out of jail free

> *The only thing you can do wrong in agile is doing things the same way as you did three months ago. Always be learning, always be experimenting and changing.*

Some of the suggestions made in this book might not be acceptable to people in your organization. As with agile, you need to find your own way to OKRs. You can listen to sage advice, read esteemed books and copy best practice, but ultimately you have to find what works in your culture.

Be prepared to experiment. If it helps, consider every word in this book as a thesis to be tested through your own experimentation.

The truth is that while there may be hard and fast rules about OKRs at the likes of Google and Intel, most organizations are a long way from such rules. Anyone who claims to know about OKRs – including me – is retelling their experience gained in a particular context. Your context is almost certainly different.

When OKRs are combined with agile the people doing the work – like you – also have a say in how things work. Not only does agile push authority down to people, but agile allows – even mandates – that those doing the work have a voice in how the work is done. Agile allows itself to be modified. When OKRs are introduced to an agile environment one should expect their usage to change.

Therefore experiment with how your draft you OKRs, how you state measurements, how you document them, how you share and just about everything else. If people don't like it they will tell you and you won't do it again.

In the event that your company has chosen to make this book company lore, please use this section as your 'get out of jail free' card to break any rule.

Finally

This book is written, produced and published by myself, Allan Kelly, through my company Software Strategy (once known as *Allan Kelly Associates*). That means I am responsible for all the 'mistakes'.

I like to think I'm good at expressing myself in my native language, but frankly spelling, punctuation, grammar and such is not my strong point. Despite a professional copy-edit some mistakes will slip through.

If you have any comments or observations about this book, or have OKR stories to share, please contact me, I am allan@allankelly.net.

ISBNs

Succeeding with Agile & OKRs, second edition, 2023

Print: 978-1-912832-25-5 Amazon

Print: 978-1-912832-30-9 second source

Electronic: 978-1-912832-26-2 ePub

Electronic: 978-1-912832-27-9 PDF

Audio: 978-1-912832-31-6

First edition, 2021: 978-1-912832-06-4 (print), 978-1-912832-08-8 (ePub)

Please review

If you enjoyed *Succeeding with OKRs in Agile* please consider leaving a short online review[1] on your favourite site to help others.

The author will be very grateful!

---

[1] https://amzn.to/47GVDki

Further reading

OKRs

Measure what Matters, John Doerr, 2017

5 Ways Your Company May Be Misusing OKRs, Itamar Gilad, https://itamargilad.com/5-ways-your-company-may-be-misusing-okrs/, accessed July 2020

Measuring

How to Measure Anything, Douglas W Hubbard, 2010, John Wiley and Sons

Competitive Engineering, Tom Gilb, 2005, Elsevier Butterworth–Heinemann

Problems with measurement and targets

Goodhart's Law, Charles Goodhart, https://en.wikipedia.org/wiki/Goodhart's_law, accessed July 2020

Obliquity, John Kay, 2011

The Tyranny of Metrics, Jerry Z Muller, 2018

Agile and teams

Right to Left: The Digital Leader's Guide to Lean and Agile, Mike Burrows, 2019

Amoeba Management, Kazuo Inamori, 1999

Xanpan: Team Centric Agile Software Development, Allan Kelly, 2014

Continuous Digital, Allan Kelly, 2018

Management

The Fearless Organization: Creating Psychological Safety in the Workplace for Learning, Innovation, and Growth, Amy Edmondson, 2018

Simply Managing, Henry Mintzberg, 2013

The Rise and Fall of Strategic Planning, Henry Mintzberg, 1994

Hypothesis-Driven Development, Barry O'Reilly, https://barryoreilly.com/how-to-implement-hypothesis-driven-development/

Lean Startup, Eric Ries, 2011

OKRs extra - coming soon

Less is more, so this book has tried to stay small.

But there is more to say about working with OKRs and agile. Some of that gets into thorny issues of managers, management, teams, value (just what is it?) and more. Those chapters exists, they're just not here.

To go deeper into OKRs, continue the journey with Succeeding with OKRs in Agile Extra[2] – coming soon on LeanPub. Register your interest today and be the first to know.

---

[2]https://leanpub.com/agileokrsextra

Acknowledgements

First edition

Thanks to Inga Wassenhoven, Dez Conner, Bjorn De Wael, Ramage Marzden, Inge Gordon and Frederik Van Herterijck for letting me be part of their OKR journey. Double thanks to Inga and Dez for deep discussions on the nature of OKRs and hours spent drafting and redrafting potential OKRs.

Thanks to Mike Burrows for comments and suggestions on a very early draft of this book, and thanks to an almost anonymous reader, Sam, who sent me feedback via LeanPub.

Thanks too to everyone who bought the early versions of this book, for providing the monetary feedback that showed people would find it interesting and that I should keep writing.

Second edition

One can learn so much from questions. The questions I've had since the first edition have helped me improve this book.

So thank you to everyone who has asked a question: about this book directly or on social media, in OKR consulting or training sessions, after presentations (especially *Reawakening Agile with OKRs* and *Honey, I Shrunk the Backlog.*)

And thank you to everyone who has given me the opportunities to get those questions: by invited me to speak, advise, consult or just talk about OKRs.

Also by Allan Kelly

Books to be Written: a non-fiction author's how-to guide to writing, publishing and marketing[3], Software Strategy/LeanPub, 2023

The Art of Agile Product Ownership[4], Apress, 2019

Continuous Digital: an agile alternative to projects for digital business[5], Software Strategy/LeanPub, 2018

Project Myopia[6], Software Strategy/LeanPub, 2018

Little Book of Requirements and User Stories[7], Software Strategy/LeanPub, 2017

Xanpan: Team Centric Agile Software Development[8], Software Strategy/LeanPub, 2015

Business Patterns for Software Developers[9], Wiley, 2012

EuroPLoP 2009 Proceedings of 14th European Conference on Pattern Languages of Programming, Irese Germany, July 2009

Changing Software Development: Learning to be Agile[10], John Wiley and Sons, 2008

---

[3]https://amzn.to/3DwgCsK
[4]https://amzn.to/3spqRH4
[5]https://amzn.to/2CUbMbW
[6]https://amzn.to/2wZW9JM
[7]https://amzn.to/2P6VB1K
[8]https://amzn.to/3sj0b0c
[9]https://amzn.to/3mRwZXr
[10]https://amzn.to/3sfinI5

www.ingramcontent.com/pod-product-compliance
Lightning Source LLC
Chambersburg PA
CBHW061810210326
41599CB00034B/6948